SPECIAL RECIPES *from the*

CHARLESTON CAKE LADY

OTHER BOOKS BY TERESA PREGNALL

Treasured Recipes from the Charleston Cake Lady

SPECIAL RECIPES *from the*

CHARLESTON CAKE LADY

TERESA PREGNALL

with Wally Pregnall

wm

William Morrow

An Imprint of HarperCollins*Publishers*

HarperCollins books may be purchased for educational, business, or sales promotional use. For information, please write: Special Markets Department, HarperCollins Publishers Inc., 10 East 53rd Street, New York, NY 10022.

FIRST EDITION

Designed by Leah Carlson-Stanisic

Library of Congress Cataloging-in-Publication Data has been applied for.

ISBN 0-688-17032-3

08 / QWF 10 9 8 7 6 5

For the three men in my life,
Daddy, Billy, and Wally, with enormous love

CONTENTS

Acknowledgments *ix*

Introduction *xi*

The Usual 1

The Unusual 23

New Old Friends 35

New Best-Sellers from the Charleston Cake Lady 45

Brownies, Chews, and Other Take-Alongs 65

Tasty Morning Treats 81

The "Extra-Goods" 103

In Ann's Memory 113

Index *123*

ACKNOWLEDGMENTS

THIS BOOK WOULD NOT have been possible without the generosity of my many friends who have shared their special recipes. My warmest thanks to Patricia Raad, Mary Michael Hair, Betty Rivers, Margaret Wilkes, Dee Newton, Roberta Josey, Carol Baxley, Diane Chandler, Joyce McCarrell, Quito McKenna, Linda Hardy, Maureen Frye, Mary Ann Nelson, Ann Molony, Joan Evans, Joan Budds, and Sadie Green. A big thank you to some of the other folks whose help has been invaluable. At the William Morrow group: Carrie Weinberg, Pam Hoenig, and Kate Heddings. Working with you has been a real pleasure.

Special thanks to the world's best chauffeurs, those wonderful drivers who helped me enjoy the many book signings: Eleanor Kline, Mary O'Neill, Angela O'Neill, Teresa Ann Gavitt and, of course, Wally, who is always ready to help his mom. We had fun times together.

Words cannot express my gratitude to Jennifer Williams, the delightful and charming editor who guided me through the muddy waters of "first book sailing." Her gentle help, tactful suggestions, and warm friendship gave me the courage and confidence to write this book. Jennifer has a special place in my heart.

Finally, no endeavor of mine would be successful without the help of Allison and Peggy Engel and the support of my family, Wally, Sadie, and Teresa Ann—my warmest thanks.

INTRODUCTION

WHEN I WAS ASKED to write my first book, *Treasured Recipes from the Charleston Cake Lady*, I just knew I didn't have the time to devote to such an undertaking. I was simply too busy. But the challenge was great and I decided to accept the offer. Now my lifestyle has become even busier and sometimes I ask myself, "Just how busy can one old lady be?" But it's been fun; I enjoy the work and have loved meeting all the wonderful folks that I didn't know before the book was written. You'll hear all about these folks throughout the book because that's what this book is all about—sharing with you the wonderful ideas and recipes that have come my way from these special people.

I look back over the past few years with wonder and gratitude. It is one of the world's great wonders that I was able to enter and exit the publishing world without incident. The gratitude I have is for the opportunity to meet and enjoy so many delightful people and to form such lovely friendships. These have been very meaningful years for Wally and me, and to those who made it possible, we offer our best thanks.

Just a few words now about my experiences in the publishing world, a whole new world for me. Very shortly after I signed the contract for my first book with William Morrow in March 1996, an editor was assigned to me. It took her several months and a number of revisions to decide the format that she preferred for my recipes. After trying to accommodate her a number of times, I finally went back to the original format and that was exactly what she wanted! Since it was right about this time that my best friend, Ann Stender Gilmore, was diagnosed with terminal cancer, I had little time for, or contact with my editor. Ann's illness and death consumed so much of my time, energy, and love that it was not until after her untimely death in October that I was able get back into the writing mode to begin my manuscript. When the manuscript was finished and delivered before my January deadline, I wasn't sure if it would suit the editor, since she had not seen any of the intervening work (she had told me not to send anything until the entire manuscript was completed). I wasn't surprised that she wasn't too happy with my finished manuscript; indeed, I began to get the feeling that she really had little interest in my book. She left the company shortly thereafter, and it was my next editor, Jennifer Williams, who enthusiastically engineered the successful completion of my first cookbook endeavor.

As soon as the book was published, there began a flurry of activity that in many ways was the genesis of the present book. Ann Burger, Charleston's fabulous food editor, wrote a stellar article about *Treasured Recipes*, complete with excerpts and recipes from the book, as well as pictures of many of the cakes. Susan Davis and her devoted staff staged a sellout book signing at Chapter Two Bookstore, the first of many book signings in the Charleston area. Right away we began receiving offers for favorite or family recipes, interesting stories, and always the query, "When can we expect your next book?" With such an impetus it was time to seriously think about a second book.

The Charleston Cake Lady continues to be busy in the bakery. We have developed some new cakes and sent many of them all over the country. One was featured in the *Victoria* magazine newsletter and another one made it to Universal City to be shown on the *Home and Family* show. All the new cakes are in this book, as well as several chapters of what I like to call "different" cakes. Ann had an expression which she often used and at times would let me use also. When an item or story was something she had heard or seen before, she always called it "Same-o, same-o!" So in this book I have tried very hard (with the exception of our beloved pound cakes) to avoid the "same-o's."

You won't find many cakes in this book that require frosting. There are several reasons for this, the first being that almost all of our cakes are so moist, they need no frosting. Each one is rich and tasty in its own way and usually needs nothing more than a fork or spoon to enjoy. The other reason is that even though I can whip up a bowl of frosting without much thought these days, it wasn't always that way. I have been known to have problems with frostings—or at least with the actual frosting of the cake. One such incident has never been forgotten.

It happened a number of years ago when my son Wally was a grade-school student. It seems the school or the parent-teacher association was always having some kind of sale. There was an annual school bazaar and always a cake booth. (I don't hear much about school bazaars anymore; either they have gone out of style or I'm too old to be involved.) At any rate, the cake booth needed cakes and I set out to do my part. Since I had not at that time learned the trick of baking the cake and freezing it before frosting it, I got up early on the morning of the bazaar and started my production. Three devil's food layers were soon cooling on the kitchen table waiting to be frosted—this was going to be a special cake. The caramel frosting was a success, and it really didn't take long to put the cake together; I was on schedule, or so I thought. When this fairly nice-looking three-layer cake was finished I put it on the sink drainboard and went on to my other chores.

As I said, this was a number of years ago—in the days before any of us had swimming pools and fences. Our neighborhood was a friendly place. Our next door neighbors, Julie Ann and Eddie Trouche, were especially friendly (they still are), and we were often in and out of each other's houses. That Saturday morning Eddie wandered into the kitchen looking for Billy, my husband. I knew nothing until I heard peals of laughter from the other end of the house. By the time I reached the kitchen, Eddie was doubled over. The top layer of my school bazaar cake was in the sink; the second layer was on its way down. Of course, I joined in the laughter as we called in anyone we could find to see this spectacle. We were able to salvage only the bottom layer, and I learned instantly that the cooling process is a vital part of cake making. Although Julie Ann and Eddie are no longer our neighbors, we still laugh at ourselves, and I doubt that we will ever forget that Saturday morning with the school bazaar cake.

By now, I'm sure you are convinced that the production of *Treasured Recipes* was a rewarding experience. Among the blessings for which I am particularly grateful is having such a wide circle of friends, as well as the many invitations so graciously extended. Peggy Engel's invitation to speak at a food seminar at the Smithsonian Institution in March 1999 was certainly one of the finer moments I have known.

In the pages that follow, I hope you will read along with the Charleston Cake Lady as we create more cakes, sign books, meet new folks, and enjoy the fellowship that accompanies the sharing of our baking feats with one another. You will come across a few names more than once, so at the risk of suggesting a cast of characters, I'll introduce some of them to you now. Wally is my son. He appears often since he is a vital part of the Charleston Cake Lady operation. He is a soft-spoken, gentle young man who really does not walk on water—his mother just thinks he does. Billy was my husband. Before his death in 1993 he was very involved not only in the bakery but in every aspect of our lives. He was the very core of our family life and his spirit will always be with us. Sadie Green, our housekeeper, is the one who keeps us straight. She backs down from no one, leaving little doubt as to who is in charge here. Since she passed her fiftieth anniversary with us years ago, who are we to question her authority? Teresa Ann Gavitt is my niece. She and her husband, Lee, live in Florida—much too far away for folks we love so dearly. Mary Michael Hair, who is mentioned many times, is a wonderful friend whose recipes are not to be missed.

Please feel free to call me if you have a question, a problem, a suggestion, or just for a visit. I look forward to hearing from you.

THE USUAL

To CALL OUR BELOVED pound cakes "usual" is not an insult; rather, it is a compliment of sorts. We eat and enjoy pound cake so routinely that we simply think of it as "usual." Daddy's brother used to say that no other cake was fit to eat! Of course, I don't agree with that comment, but I do believe that my uncle's assessment of pound cakes was from his heart. In the next few pages you will find a few pound cakes, perhaps just a bit different from those in *Treasured Recipes* but, we think, just as delicious and certainly just as easy to make.

Several of these pound cake recipes are Charleston Cake

Lady creations, and several have been given to me by very special people. The 7UP Pound Cake is a gift from Dee Newton, one of my Charleston friends who now lives in Georgia. Her cake has become one of my favorite pound cakes, and Wally's friends rave about it, too, so it rates very high on our list.

The German Chocolate Pound Cake recipe was given to me by Patricia Raad, who lives in Charlotte, North Carolina. Patricia bought a copy of *Treasured Recipes,* began baking some of the recipes, and called to say how much she was enjoying the book. We had a most enjoyable telephone visit, the first of many to follow, and have since formed a real friendship. We visit frequently by telephone, and each of us looks forward to our next visit. Patricia appears several times in this book, and such a delightful appearance she makes! Her recipe "finds" are fantastic, and I'm sure you will enjoy them almost as much as I have enjoyed Patricia.

You are probably ready now to stop reading and start baking, so I won't hold you much longer. Here are just a few brief suggestions about pound cakes before you start:

- Use an electric mixer, if at all possible, since it is absolutely necessary to cream the butter and sugar well.

- Even though I prefer to use real butter in my pound cakes, you may substitute margarine in most cases—

but be sure that you're using real margarine. The light, reduced-fat, or fat-free varieties contain high percentages of water and/or oil, thereby reducing the moistness of the cake. Real margarine is hard to find these days, so read the labels very carefully, or use butter.

- Some of my pound cakes are placed in a cold oven. There are many bakers who disagree with me, claiming that they have better luck using a preheated oven. Since the use of a cold oven is nowhere carved in stone, by all means do what is best for you. Many of the Charleston Cake Lady pound cakes are placed in a cold oven since this works best for me.

- Although the use of vegetable cooking spray is recommended in many recipes, I prefer to grease and flour the pan for my pound cakes. You may use any fresh, solid vegetable shortening, then sprinkle the greased coating with a light dusting of flour.

- Always, but always test for doneness. Do this for every cake you bake, but most especially for pound cakes. Insert a cake tester into the center of the cake. If it comes out clean, the cake is done. If it needs to bake longer, increase the cooking time in five-minute intervals, testing for doneness each time.

GERMAN CHOCOLATE
POUND CAKE

Of all the wonderful Patricia Raad recipe contributions, this is one of my favorites and my customers rave about it. I don't tell them that it is made with a mix and that the frosting is baked in the cake. Moist, rich, dense, and absolutely delicious, this German chocolate pound cake of Patricia's is one of the easiest cakes I've ever made. I'm sure you will agree with me, and I'm also sure that you will have calls for seconds.

Shortening for greasing the Bundt pan
One 18.25-ounce package German chocolate cake mix
¼ cup vegetable oil
1 cup water
3 large eggs
One 15-ounce container coconut pecan frosting

Preheat the oven to 350°F. Grease a 12-cup Bundt pan.

In a large mixing bowl, mix the cake mix, oil, water, and eggs together with an electric mixer on low speed until the ingredients are well distributed, about 1 minute. Scrape the bottom of the bowl with a spatula and beat for 2 minutes, still on low speed. Add the container of frosting and continue beating on low speed for about 2 minutes.

Pour the batter into the prepared pan and bake until a cake tester inserted in the center of the cake comes out clean, 55 to 60 minutes. Let the cake cool in the pan. Invert the cooled cake onto a plate and allow it to cool thoroughly before slicing. No frosting is needed—it's already in the cake.

MAKES 18 TO 20 SLICES

SADIE'S CHOICE
POUND CAKE

Our renowned housekeeper, Sadie Green, has very definite eating habits. She is hard to please and it isn't often that she actually likes something new. So when there's even a glimmer of hope for her approval in our bakery, I begin to celebrate. Since pound cake is her favorite, she was happy to sample this new one and was ready with her comments. To my surprise, she found no fault with this cake (of course, I didn't mention the buttermilk since she doesn't like buttermilk). After a few minor adjustments, we had another taste test and Sadie proclaimed this one to be the best yet. What an accolade!

The ingredients in this pound cake differ only slightly from some others, but it is the easiest one I have ever baked, and I do believe that Sadie's assessment of it is a good one. She's quite pleased to have it named for her.

Shortening and all-purpose flour for greasing the
   tube pan
2½ cups all-purpose flour
1 cup self-rising flour
1½ cups (3 sticks) butter (do not substitute margarine)
3 cups granulated sugar

6 large eggs
1¼ cups buttermilk
1 teaspoon pure vanilla extract
1 teaspoon pure almond extract

Do not preheat the oven. Grease and flour a 12-cup tube pan.

Sift the flours together into a medium-size mixing bowl and set aside.

In a large mixing bowl, mix the butter and sugar together with an electric mixer on low speed for about 7 minutes. Add the eggs one at a time, mixing well after each addition. Alternately add the flour mixture and the buttermilk. Mix in the vanilla and almond extracts.

Set the oven to 325°F. Pour the batter into the prepared pan and bake until a cake tester inserted in the center of the cake comes out clean, about 70 minutes. (This is a very large cake, so be sure to test in the middle of the cake.) Let the cake cool in the pan. Invert the cooled cake onto a plate and allow it to cool thoroughly before slicing.　MAKES 25 SLICES

MARBLED POUND CAKE

If the baker is allowed to have a favorite, mine would be Mar-
bled Pound Cake. For some unknown reason, however, I've never
enjoyed dropping spoonfuls of chocolate batter onto white batter,
then swirling with a knife. So even though I enjoy eating a mar-
bled cake, it is not much fun for me to bake one. When one of my
special customers, Carol Baxley, sent me her recipe, I was sur-
prised and delighted—no more dropping spoonfuls and swirling.
Her version is as light in texture as it is delicious in taste, and
since it is so rich and moist it needs no frosting or accompaniment.

Shortening and all-purpose flour for greasing the
   tube pan
1½ cups (3 sticks) butter (do not substitute margarine)
2¼ cups granulated sugar
6 large eggs, separated
3 cups self-rising flour, sifted
¾ cup milk
1½ teaspoons pure vanilla extract
One 16-ounce can chocolate syrup

Do not preheat the oven. Grease and flour a 12-cup tube pan.
   In a large mixing bowl, cream the butter and sugar
together with an electric mixer on low speed until the mixture

is light and fluffy, 5 to 6 minutes. Add the egg yolks one at a time, blending well after each addition. Alternately add the flour and milk and beat until well blended. Clean and completely dry the beaters of the mixer.

In a separate large mixing bowl, beat the egg whites with the mixer on high speed until stiff peaks form, then gently fold them into the batter.

Set the oven to 300°F.

Pour one-third of the batter into a medium-size mixing bowl and stir in the chocolate syrup. Set aside.

Pour half of the remaining white batter into the prepared pan. Pour in the chocolate batter. Then pour the remaining white batter on top. Bake until a cake tester inserted in the center of the cake comes out clean, about 1 hour and 50 minutes.

Allow the cake to cool in the pan for at least 1 hour. Transfer the cake to a pretty cake plate and prepare to enjoy the rave reviews. MAKES 25 GENEROUS SLICES

7UP POUND CAKE

A number of years ago, the 7UP Cake made its debut. It was made with a prepared cake mix and for some reason it did not appeal to me. When Dee Newton recently gave me her recipe "from scratch," I couldn't wait to try it. I was pleasantly surprised. This light, moist, lemony cake literally melts in your mouth, and I'm grateful to Dee for her delicious new pound cake.

Shortening and all-purpose flour for greasing the
    tube pan
1 cup (2 sticks) butter (do not substitute margarine)
½ cup vegetable oil
3 cups granulated sugar
5 large eggs
3 cups all-purpose flour, sifted
1 cup 7UP
1 teaspoon pure vanilla extract
1 teaspoon pure lemon extract

Do not preheat the oven. Grease and flour a 12-cup tube pan.

In a large mixing bowl, beat the butter, oil, and sugar together with an electric mixer on low speed until the mixture is creamy, about 4 minutes. Add the eggs one at a time, beating well after each addition. Alternately add the sifted flour and the 7UP. Mix well. Mix in the vanilla and lemon extracts.

Set the oven to 300°F. Pour the batter into the prepared pan and bake until a cake tester inserted in the center of the cake comes out clean, about 90 minutes. Let the cake cool in the pan. Invert the cooled cake onto a plate and allow it to cool thoroughly before slicing. MAKES 20 SLICES

WHITE CHOCOLATE
POUND CAKE

Being the town's biggest chocolate addict (dark chocolate, that is), I always thought that I hadn't met a piece of chocolate that I didn't like. Until I met white chocolate. It just wasn't the same as dark chocolate, and I had no interest in it. Last year, however, I decided that white chocolate was a challenge and that surely it could find its place in my bakery. So, after a number of trials, the White Chocolate Pound Cake emerged. It has a distinctive flavor, but the white chocolate is so subtle most folks try to guess what the flavor is. It has even been called the "mystery pound cake" by some of my customers. But it's no mystery. It is just very, very good, and because it is so rich and moist, it needs no accompaniment.

Shortening and all-purpose flour for greasing the tube
  pan
One 6-ounce bar good-quality white chocolate
  (morsels do not perform as well as the solid bar does
  in this recipe)
3 cups all-purpose flour
1 teaspoon baking powder
½ teaspoon salt
¼ teaspoon baking soda

1 cup (2 sticks) butter (do not substitute margarine)
2 cups granulated sugar
5 large eggs
1 cup sour cream
1 teaspoon pure vanilla extract
1 teaspoon pure almond extract

Do not preheat the oven. Grease and flour a 12-cup tube pan.

Melt the chocolate in the top of a double boiler over simmering water or in a microwave oven (2 to 3 minutes on low will melt the chocolate) and let it cool. Sift together the flour, baking powder, salt, and baking soda into a medium-size mixing bowl. Set aside.

In a large mixing bowl, cream the butter and sugar together with an electric mixer until light and fluffy, about 5 minutes. Add the eggs one at a time, mixing for 1 minute after each addition. Stir in the cooled white chocolate and blend well. Alternately add the dry ingredients and the sour cream. Mix in the vanilla and almond extracts.

Pour the batter into the prepared pan. Place in a cold oven and set the oven to 300°F. Bake until a cake tester inserted in the center of the cake comes out clean, about 1 hour. Allow the cake to cool in the pan for about 1 hour. Place the cake on a cake rack and let it cool for several hours before slicing.

MAKES 22 SLICES

EVAPORATED MILK
POUND CAKE

As pound cakes go, this one is probably one of the best. It is most certainly one of the easiest to make. The increased measure of baking powder produces an extremely light cake, and the evaporated milk mixes well with the flavorings for a pleasant taste.

Shortening and all-purpose flour for greasing the
    tube pan
3 cups all-purpose flour
3 teaspoons baking powder
3 cups granulated sugar
1½ cups (3 sticks) butter or margarine
5 large eggs
1 cup evaporated milk
1 teaspoon pure vanilla extract
1 teaspoon pure almond extract

Do not preheat the oven. Grease and flour a 12-cup tube pan.

Sift together the flour, baking powder, and sugar into a medium-size mixing bowl. In a large mixing bowl, cream the butter with an electric mixer on low speed for about 1 minute. Add the eggs, one at a time, beating well after each addition.

Alternately add the flour mixture and evaporated milk, beating well after each addition. Mix in the vanilla and almond extracts.

Pour the batter into the prepared pan and set the oven to 325°F. Bake until a cake tester inserted in the center of the cake comes out clean, about 1 hour and 15 minutes. Let the cake cool in the pan. Invert the cooled cake onto a plate and allow it to cool thoroughly before slicing.

MAKES 20 SLICES

AIR FORCE APPLE
POUND CAKE

*One of my most pleasant experiences in recent years has been my
association with the Williams-Sonoma–Greenville people. At a
book signing there in June 1998, I met a most delightful group—
the staff. Their warmth and friendliness afforded me a lovely
afternoon, and I left with an equally lovely trio of new friends.*

*Since that time, that trio—Diane Chandler, Joyce McCar-
rell, and Quito McKenna—and I have kept in touch with one
another. We have also shared our recipes, and with their permis-
sion I have included a few of their favorites for you. They have
become favorites in this house, so I know you will enjoy them.*

*This first recipe is Quito's cake. He calls it "so simple and so
yummy," and he's so right. It is truly yummy. His wife baked it
for newcomers to the base when they were in the Air Force. Can
you imagine a nicer welcome?*

Shortening for greasing the Bundt pan
3 cups granulated sugar
3 cups all-purpose flour
1 teaspoon ground cinnamon
1 teaspoon baking powder
1 teaspoon baking soda

1½ teaspoons salt
¾ cup vegetable oil
2 large eggs, beaten
1 teaspoon pure vanilla extract
1 cup coarsely chopped walnuts
4 cups peeled, cored, and diced tart apples

Preheat the oven to 350°F. Grease a 12-cup Bundt pan. Using about ½ cup granulated sugar, coat the pan heavily.

Sift together the flour, cinnamon, baking powder, baking soda, and salt into a medium-size mixing bowl. Add the remaining sugar and set aside.

In a large mixing bowl, use a spoon to blend the oil, eggs, and vanilla together. Add the dry ingredients and mix well. Mix in the walnuts and apples and stir gently.

Pour the batter into the prepared pan and bake until a cake tester inserted in the center of the cake comes out clean, about 1 hour. Let the cake cool completely in the pan. Invert onto a plate and cool thoroughly before slicing.

MAKES 20 SLICES

SUMAMA'S BUTTERMILK
POUND CAKE

Diane Chandler graciously offered me her grandmother's butter-milk pound cake recipe and I am most grateful. The mixing of this cake veers somewhat from the norm, but it works and it is delicious. The directions call for a tube pan and that's what I use; however, Diane says that she makes this cake in layers, as well as sheet cake style. Perhaps we should rename it Sumama's Versatile Buttermilk Cake!

Shortening and all-purpose flour for greasing the
    tube pan
3 cups all-purpose flour
½ teaspoon salt
½ teaspoon baking soda
¾ cup (1½ sticks) margarine or butter
2 cups granulated sugar
1 cup buttermilk
3 large eggs
1 teaspoon pure vanilla extract

Preheat the oven to 350°F. Grease and flour a 12-cup tube pan.

Sift together the flour, salt, and baking soda into a medium-size mixing bowl. Set aside.

In a large mixing bowl, cream the margarine (or butter) and sugar together with an electric mixer on high speed, about 5 minutes. Reduce the speed to medium-low. Add the butter-milk, then the dry ingredients. Add the eggs, one at a time, mixing thoroughly after each addition. Mix in the vanilla.

Pour the batter into the prepared pan and bake until a cake tester inserted in the center of the cake comes out clean, about 1 hour. Let the cake cool in the pan. Invert the cake onto a plate and allow it to cool thoroughly before slicing.

MAKES 18 TO 20 SLICES

NOTE: This unusual mixing procedure makes a good cake texture that is free of air bubbles.

JOYCE McCARRELL'S
BUTTERMILK POUND CAKE

It's easy to see why Joyce says this is the cake she does best. She also reports that she has been baking this cake since her teens, and that's easy to see, too. I believe that even a preteen would find it fun to bake this cake, since the mixing of it has to be the simplest I've come across. To be honest, the use of Crisco instead of butter raised an eyebrow, but only for a short time—until I tried it myself. It is now one of my favorites!

Here's the McCarrell family story: According to Joyce, the cake is delicious served warm, so while the cake was baking, she, her dad, her brother, and sister would literally sit around the kitchen table waiting for it to be done. Then they would each have a big glass of milk and pretty much demolish the cake. If by chance there was any cake left, they toasted it for breakfast.

It will be interesting to know how your family treats this gem.

Shortening and all-purpose flour for greasing the
   tube pan
3 cups all-purpose flour
2 cups granulated sugar
½ teaspoon salt
½ teaspoon baking soda

½ teaspoon baking powder
1 cup Crisco vegetable shortening (use no substitute)
1 cup buttermilk
4 large eggs, well beaten
1 teaspoon pure vanilla extract

Preheat the oven to 325°F. Grease and flour a 12-cup tube pan.

Into a large mixing bowl, sift together the flour, sugar, salt, baking soda, and baking powder. All at once stir in the shortening, buttermilk, eggs, and vanilla. Beat on low speed with an electric mixer until all of the ingredients are well blended, 4 to 5 minutes.

Pour the batter into the prepared pan and bake for 60 to 75 minutes, testing after 60 minutes for doneness. A cake tester inserted in the center of the cake should come out clean. Let the cake cool in the pan (unless you act like the McCarrell family and dig right in!). Invert onto a plate, slice, and serve.

MAKES 20 SLICES

THE UNUSUAL

Perhaps the cakes in this chapter are not really "unusual," but their ingredients do indeed differ from the norm. I had never tried an Orange Marmalade Cake until Patricia Raad gave me her recipe. We thought it was delicious (even Sadie liked it!), and it makes a grand dessert for a big crowd. Mary Michael Hair's Blackberry Jam Cake is the kind that almost makes my mouth water just thinking about it. And the Beer Cake catches everyone's eye, as well as their taste buds. You won't find any "same-o's" here, and I hope you will be pleased with each selection.

ORANGE MARMALADE CAKE

Another gift from Patricia Raad. Her desserts finds are phe-nomonal and this one is no exception. I hope Patricia will not object to the few changes I have made, and I hope you will enjoy this super-rich, easy-to-make dessert. Take one to your next covered-dish party and be prepared to share the recipe.

FOR THE TOPPING
  Cooking spray for greasing the cake pan
  One 12-ounce jar orange marmalade
  ½ cup sweetened grated coconut
  ¼ cup (½ stick) butter, melted
FOR THE CAKE
  4 large eggs, separated
  1 cup (2 sticks) butter or margarine, softened
  2 cups granulated sugar
  3 cups all-purpose flour, sifted
  1 cup orange juice

Grease a 13 × 9-inch pan. In a medium-size mixing bowl, mix the orange marmalade, coconut, and melted butter together. Pour into the prepared pan and set aside.

Preheat the oven to 350°F. In a medium-size mixing bowl, beat the egg whites with an electric mixer on high speed until they form stiff peaks. Set aside. Clean and completely dry the beaters of the mixer.

In a large mixing bowl, beat the butter and sugar together with an electric mixer on low speed for about 5 minutes. Stir in the egg yolks and mix well. Alternately add the flour and the orange juice and mix until the ingredients are well distributed. Fold in the beaten egg whites with a spatula.

Pour the batter over the orange marmalade mixture in the baking pan. Bake until a cake tester inserted in the middle of the cake comes out clean, about 30 minutes. Let the cake cool in the pan. Invert the cooled cake onto a tray or cake board and cut into squares.

MAKES TWENTY-FOUR 2-INCH SQUARES

BLACKBERRY JAM CAKE

For as long as I can remember, I heard raves about Blackberry Jam Cake but never had the opportunity to taste one. It was not until Mary Michael Hair gave me her mother's recipe a couple of years ago that I learned the reason for the raves. It is a truly delicious cake and one which will make any occasion a special one.

Shortening and all-purpose flour for greasing the
   tube pan
3¼ cups all-purpose flour
1 teaspoon baking soda
1 teaspoon baking powder
1 teaspoon ground nutmeg
1 teaspoon ground allspice
1 teaspoon ground cinnamon
¾ teaspoon salt
1 cup granulated sugar
1 cup (2 sticks) butter, softened (do not use
   margarine)
4 large eggs
1 cup seedless blackberry jam
1 cup buttermilk
1⅓ cups shelled and coarsely chopped black walnuts

Do not preheat the oven. Grease and flour a 12-cup tube pan. Sift together the flour, baking soda, baking powder, nutmeg, allspice, cinnamon, and salt into a medium-size mixing bowl. Set aside.

In a large mixing bowl, beat the sugar and butter together with an electric mixer on low speed until creamy, about 5 minutes. Add the eggs one at a time, beating well after each addition. Add the blackberry jam and mix well. Alternately add the dry ingredients and the buttermilk, beating well after each addition. Stir in the walnuts.

Set the oven to 325°F. Pour the batter into the prepared pan and bake until a cake tester inserted in the center of the cake comes out clean, about 1½ hours. Let the cake cool in the pan. Invert onto a plate and allow to cool thoroughly before slicing.　MAKES 20 GENEROUS SLICES

Beer Cake

*I have no idea how the beer makes this date-nut cake so delicious.
I can simply say that it is one of the most unusual cakes we bake.
Extremely dense and moist, it needs no frosting or accompaniment
and its shelf life is quite long. It freezes well, it is a wonderful holiday cake, and just think about the healthy bonus in those dates!*

*For this little gem our thanks go to Ann Burger, Charleston's
fabulous food editor. Ann provides us with the best there is in the
food world, and I'm sure that many Charlestonians are grateful
to her—but none more so than the Charleston Cake Lady.*

Shortening and all-purpose flour for greasing the
   tube pan
3 cups all-purpose flour
1 teaspoon ground cinnamon
1 teaspoon ground allspice
½ teaspoon salt
2 teaspoons baking soda
2 cups firmly packed light brown sugar
1 cup (2 sticks) butter or margarine, softened
2 large eggs
2 cups beer, at room temperature
1½ cups coarsely chopped pecans or walnuts
2 cups chopped dates

Do not preheat the oven. Grease and flour a 12-cup tube pan.

Sift together the flour, cinnamon, allspice, and salt into a medium-size mixing bowl. Set aside.

In a large mixing bowl, sprinkle the baking soda over the sugar. Add the butter and beat with an electric mixer on low speed until smooth, 2 to 3 minutes. Add the eggs and beat well. Alternately stir in the dry ingredients and the beer. Fold in the nuts and dates and stir until all the ingredients are well distributed.

Pour the batter into the prepared pan and set the oven to 300°F. Bake until a cake tester inserted in the center of the cake comes out clean, about 1 hour and 45 minutes. Allow the cake to cool in the pan for 1½ hours. Transfer the cake to a cake plate and allow to cool thoroughly. (Be sure that the cake is thoroughly cooled before slicing.)

Makes 22 generous slices

PINEAPPLE SHEET CAKE

Have you ever hit the panic button when you learn that unexpected company is on the way? We all have at one time or another, but with these few ingredients, which you probably always keep in your pantry, you can avoid that panic attack. This cake is so easy and serves so many, it's a great standby. (Note that there's no shortening.)

Cooking spray for greasing the cake pan
2 large eggs
2 cups granulated sugar
1 teaspoon pure vanilla extract
One 20-ounce can crushed pineapple in heavy syrup
2 cups all-purpose flour
2 teaspoons baking soda
1 cup coarsely chopped pecans
Cream Cheese Icing (recipe follows)

Preheat the oven to 350°F. Grease a 13 × 9-inch pan.

In a large mixing bowl, mix the eggs, sugar, vanilla, and pineapple together with a spoon. Sift the flour and baking soda into the bowl. Mix well. Fold in the pecans.

Pour the batter into the prepared pan and bake until a cake

tester comes out clean, about 45 minutes. Let the cake cool in the pan, then frost with the Cream Cheese Icing. Cut into 2-inch squares.   MAKES 24 SQUARES

Cream Cheese Icing

One 8-ounce package cream cheese, softened
½ cup (1 stick) butter or margarine, softened
1⅓ cups confectioners' sugar
1 teaspoon pure vanilla extract

Mix the ingredients together in a medium-size mixing bowl. Beat with an electric mixer on high speed until the mixture is creamy, about 5 minutes. Spread the icing on the cooled cake.

COCONUT-PECAN-TOPPED
GERMAN CHOCOLATE CAKE

German chocolate cake has long been one of my favorites, but because the filling is so rich I've always managed to leave some on my plate. With this in mind, I decided to try a pound cake variety using some of the filling ingredients as a topping. So instead of the familiar German chocolate layer cake, this one is a bit different. It is made in a tube pan so the cake sits "right side up."

FOR THE CAKE

Shortening and all-purpose flour for greasing the
   tube pan
One 6-ounce package German sweet chocolate
3 cups all-purpose flour
½ teaspoon baking soda
½ teaspoon salt
1 cup (2 sticks) butter or margarine, softened
2 cups granulated sugar
4 large eggs
2 teaspoons pure vanilla extract
1 cup buttermilk

¾ cup (1½ sticks) butter or margarine, melted
1½ cups granulated sugar
1½ teaspoons pure vanilla extract
1 cup sweetened grated coconut
1½ cups coarsely chopped pecans
Evaporated milk as needed (5 to 6 ounces)

Do not preheat the oven. Grease and flour a 12-cup tube pan. Melt the chocolate in the top of a double boiler over simmering water or in a microwave oven. Let it cool. Sift the flour, baking soda, and salt together in a medium-size bowl. Set aside.

In a large mixing bowl, beat the butter and sugar with an electric mixer on low speed until the mixture is creamy, 3 to 4 minutes. Add the eggs, vanilla, and buttermilk and blend well. Gradually add the dry ingredients and stir until the mixture is well blended. Add the melted chocolate and blend well. Pour the batter into the prepared pan and set aside.

To make the topping, in a medium-size mixing bowl, blend the butter, sugar, and vanilla together. Stir in the coconut and pecans. Slowly add the evaporated milk, stirring well after each addition, until the mixture is thick and spreadable—be careful not to let it become too soft.

continued

Set the oven to 300°F. Top the batter with the topping. When the cake is fully "topped," place it in the oven and bake until a cake tester inserted in the center of the cake comes out clean, about 1½ hours. Let the cake cool in the pan. Invert onto a plate and allow to cool thoroughly before slicing.

MAKES 20 GENEROUS SLICES

NEW OLD FRIENDS

WHEN MY HUSBAND, BILLY, attended The Citadel as a veteran student in the 1940s and '50s, his best friends were Ford Rivers, Willy Wilkes, Dick Hair, and Bert Josey. From all accounts, they formed quite a group. And the friendships they formed were long-lasting. But as often happens in the passing of time, they grew apart. Bert, Willy, and Dick left Charleston for their respective jobs, Ford spent most of his adult life taking care of his cardiac patients, and Billy spent much of his time inspecting nuclear submarines in his capacity as a naval architect. A few years ago, Willy and Dick moved back home and Ford and Billy retired, and they suddenly had time to reconnect. Bert still lives in Savannah but never misses a chance to come to Charleston to be with his "new old friends," as he likes to call us.

These fine Citadel men have gracious wives who have shared with us their favorite dessert recipes. They are reminiscent of the wonderful times we have enjoyed together, and even though Billy is no longer with us, these new old friends always make me feel special.

I hope you will enjoy these priceless recipes as much as I have enjoyed these priceless friendships.

Margaret Wilkes's Graham Cracker Nut Cake

Willy Wilkes's wife, Margaret, has been altering her recipes to make them healthy for so long that it is now a way of life for her. But she hasn't changed this one and it is absolutely delicious. Dense, moist, and ultrarich, the Graham Cracker Nut Cake stands alone. But for an extra-special occasion, try adding this frosting.

FOR THE CAKE
Shortening and all-purpose flour for greasing the
    tube pan
1 cup (2 sticks) butter (do not substitute margarine)
One 16-ounce box dark brown sugar
½ cup granulated sugar
6 large eggs
1 tablespoon baking powder
1 teaspoon salt
1½ cups sweetened grated coconut (optional)
1 teaspoon pure vanilla extract
1 pound graham cracker crumbs
2 cups finely chopped pecans

continued

FOR THE FROSTING (OPTIONAL)
½ cup (1 stick) butter or margarine, softened
One 16-ounce box confectioners' sugar
One 8-ounce can crushed pineapple, well drained
1 teaspoon pure vanilla extract
1 cup chopped pecans

Preheat the oven to 275°F. Grease and flour a 12-cup tube pan.

In a large mixing bowl, beat the butter and sugars together with an electric mixer on low speed until the mixture is creamy, about 5 minutes. Add the eggs one at a time, beating well after each addition. Mix in the baking powder, salt, coconut, and vanilla, then stir in the cracker crumbs. Fold in the nuts and gently mix well.

Pour the batter into the prepared pan and bake until a cake tester inserted in the center of the cake comes out clean, about 2 hours. Let the cake cool in the pan.

Make the frosting, if using. In a large mixing bowl, beat the butter and sugar together with an electric mixer on medium-high speed until creamy, 5 to 7 minutes. Add the well-drained pineapple, vanilla, and nuts and mix on low speed for 2 minutes. Spread on the cake when it is thoroughly cooled. MAKES 18 TO 20 SLICES

MARY MICHAEL HAIR'S PECAN PRALINE CAKE

Dick Hair's wife, Mary Michael, does everything with the greatest of ease, her baking accomplishments included. Once a year when the ladies of Christ Church in Mt. Pleasant serve their series of luncheons in the parish tearoom to benefit their many charities, Mary Michael becomes Queen of Desserts. At least, that's the name I've given her. This Pecan Praline Cake is one of her specialties, and fabulously delicious just begins to describe it. Since it is almost as easy to make as it is delicious to enjoy, it will probably become one of your specialties too.

FOR THE CAKE
  Cooking spray for greasing the cake pan
  2 cups all-purpose flour
  2 heaping tablespoons unsweetened cocoa powder
  1 teaspoon baking soda
  1 cup buttermilk
  ½ cup (1 stick) butter (do not substitute margarine)
  2 cups firmly packed light brown sugar
  2 large eggs
  1 tablespoon pure vanilla extract

continued

FOR THE ICING

½ cup (1 stick) butter, melted (do not substitute
   margarine)
1 cup firmly packed dark brown sugar
6 tablespoons whipping cream
1 cup finely chopped pecans

Preheat the oven to 350°F. Grease a 13 × 9-inch pan.

Sift together the flour, cocoa, and baking soda into a medium-size mixing bowl. Set aside. In the top of a double boiler over simmering water or on the Low setting on your microwave oven, warm the buttermilk and butter together until the butter is melted. Transfer to a large mixing bowl and add the brown sugar and eggs. Beat well with an electric mixer on low speed, about 2 minutes. Add the dry ingredients and beat well. Stir in the vanilla. Pour the batter into the prepared pan and bake until a cake tester comes out clean, 20 to 25 minutes.

Heat the oven to Broil. Mix the melted butter, brown sugar, whipping cream, and pecans together in a medium-size mixing bowl and spread the icing on top of the hot cake. Place the cake pan on the second or third rack under the broiler. Allow the icing to cook until it bubbles and is light in color (about 5 minutes—watch closely!). Cut into squares and serve warm with a dollop of whipped cream.

MAKES TWENTY-FOUR 2-INCH SQUARES

ROBERTA JOSEY'S SAVANNAH CHEWS

It probably never occurred to any of us here in Charleston that there were any other chews in the world and if there were, certainly they could never equal our Charleston chews. But along came Roberta's chews from Savannah (she's Bert Josey's wife) and a whole new dimension was added to the lowly chew. They're easy and we think they're great!

Cooking spray for greasing the cake pan
2 cups light brown sugar (not packed)
½ cup (1 stick) butter or margarine, softened
2 large eggs
1 cup all-purpose flour
1 scant teaspoon baking powder
1 teaspoon pure vanilla extract
1 cup coarsely chopped nuts or chopped dates
4 teaspoons confectioners' sugar for dusting

Preheat the oven to 325°F. Grease a 13 × 9-inch pan.

In a large mixing bowl, mix the sugar and butter with an electric mixer on low speed until the mixture is creamy, about 2 minutes. Add the eggs and beat well. Sift the flour and baking powder together into the bowl and mix well. Stir in the vanilla and the nuts.

Pour the batter into the prepared pan and bake until lightly brown on top, 20 to 25 minutes. Do not overbake. Remove from the oven and sprinkle with confectioners' sugar. Allow the chews to cool completely in the pan. Cut into squares.

MAKES TWENTY-FOUR 2-INCH SQUARES

BETTY RIVERS'S RUM CAKE

When Betty offered to share her mother's, Louise Dufour's, rum cake recipe with us, and her husband, Ford, hurriedly announced that it was superb, I knew we were in for a treat. I've eaten those so-called rum cakes that ran the gamut a few years back, but not one of them in any way resembled this real thing. It is absolutely delicious. Ford was right—it is superb. I can already guess that you will be planning a dessert party real soon to serve Mrs. Dufour's rum cake.

FOR THE CAKE
  Cooking spray for greasing the tube pan
  1 cup (2 sticks) butter (do not substitute margarine)
  2 cups granulated sugar
  6 large eggs
  2 cups all-purpose flour, sifted
  1 teaspoon salt
  3 tablespoons rum (light or dark)
  1 cup pecans, finely chopped

FOR THE RUM GLAZE
  ⅓ cup rum (light or dark) plus enough water to equal
    ½ cup liquid
  1 cup granulated sugar
  1 tablespoon butter (do not substitute margarine)

continued

Do not preheat the oven. Grease a 12-cup tube or Bundt pan.

In a large mixing bowl, beat the butter and sugar together with an electric mixer on low speed until creamy, about 5 minutes. Add 3 of the eggs, one at a time, beating well after each addition. Add 1 cup of the flour and mix well. Add the salt, then add the remaining 3 eggs, one at a time, beating well after each addition. Alternately add the remaining 1 cup flour with the rum.

Set the oven to 325°F. Sprinkle the pecans evenly in the bottom of the prepared pan. Pour the batter into the pan and bake until a cake tester inserted in the center of the cake comes out clean, about 55 minutes.

Ten minutes before the cake is finished, prepare the glaze. Put the rum/water mixture, sugar, and butter in a saucepan. Bring to a boil and let boil for 2 to 3 minutes. Pour this mixture over the hot cake. Let the cake cool in the pan. When the cake is thoroughly cooled, invert it onto a pretty plate and serve.   MAKES 18 TO 20 SLICES

NEW BEST-SELLERS *from the* CHARLESTON CAKE LADY

IN THIS GROUP OF newcomers you are certain to find one that appeals to you. The Eggnog Cake, the Victoria, and the Heavenly Chocolate have all won national acclaim, and the others have won places of honor with our customers. Since they are all easy to make and easy to ship, I'll pass along to you our shipping tips just in case you would like to send one of your culinary feats to a special someone.

You will need a corrugated box that can hold 200 pounds. This can be purchased at a packaging store. Always wrap and double wrap the cake, then either gift wrap it with heavy gift-wrapping paper or place the cake in a sturdy plastic bag. This is to prevent it from being disfigured by the packaging material. Use Styrofoam popcorn or peanuts or other suitable packaging material, enough to prevent the cake from moving in the box during shipment.

Your mailing label is very important. It must contain your return address, the name and address of the recipient, and the recipient's telephone number, including area code. Be absolutely sure that the zip code is complete and correct. I have learned that in the shipping industry the zip code is of the utmost importance. One little error and your package can be lost for days! Cover the mailing label with clear sealing tape to prevent smudging or detachment. Many of the packaging stations will package your item for you, but the fee is usually hefty, so it's smart to ready it yourself.

There are a number of shipping services available. I recommend UPS and Federal Express very highly. We don't use Federal Express as often because a large volume of our shipments are sent by ground delivery and FedEx ships only by air. The U.S. Postal Service offers dependable service also but has no pickup service. The bulk of our shipping is done with UPS and we have been consistently pleased. We have recently gone on-line with UPS and are happy with the time saved, especially during peak times.

Now that you've learned how easy it is to bake, pack, and ship a cake, your next gift dilemma is already solved. We frequently receive calls from folks who have received an unexpected cake package, and their delight is always great. You can delight someone today!

EGGNOG CAKE

When our Eggnog Cake was mentioned in the November 1997 issue of Metropolitan Home *magazine, our phones rang mercilessly. We didn't dare tell anyone that the cake contained no eggnog—that it had been given its name by Rosemary Holst, a dear friend, who insisted that it tasted like eggnog! We simply filled all the orders and enjoyed the rave reviews. It continues to be a highly popular cake. Be prepared to serve extras since it is especially light in texture.*

Cooking spray for greasing the Bundt pan
½ cup coarsely chopped pecans
One 18.25-ounce package butter recipe golden
   cake mix
⅓ cup granulated sugar
½ tablespoon ground nutmeg
1 cup sour cream
⅔ cup vegetable oil
4 large eggs

Preheat the oven to 350°F. Spray a 12-cup Bundt pan with vegetable cooking spray. Sprinkle the pecans evenly in the bottom of the pan.

Combine the cake mix, sugar, nutmeg, sour cream, oil, and eggs in a large mixing bowl and blend with an electric mixer on low speed for 1 minute. Increase the speed to medium-high and beat for 4 minutes.

Pour the batter into the prepared pan and bake until a cake tester inserted in the middle of the cake comes out clean, 45 to 50 minutes. Let the cake cool in the pan.

Invert the cake onto a pretty cake plate. The nuts form a "crown" on this special holiday cake.

MAKES 18 TO 20 SLICES

HEAVENLY CHOCOLATE CAKE

When Eric Mathis called in January 1998, asking for a chocolate cake for his Home and Family Valentine segment, I had just made the final changes to my newest chocolate creation—not yet named. We sent the unnamed cake to Universal City for their tasting pleasure and were happily surprised to learn that it would be included in the show. Our toll-free number was flashed on the screen while the cake was being shown, causing an immediate barrage of phone calls which lasted for days. Needless to say, we were busy, but it was an exciting kind of busy.

The cake was ultimately named by one of our customers, and no one has yet argued that is not heavenly. With its mocha chocolate base, milk chocolate pieces, semisweet chocolate chips, and taste of almond, it has never met a stranger who didn't like it. We had to agree that its name was perfect.

Cooking spray for greasing the Bundt pan
One 18.25-ounce package chocolate mocha cake mix
    (I like to use Duncan Hines)
⅓ cup granulated sugar
1 tablespoon all-purpose flour, unsifted
1 cup sour cream

⅔ cup vegetable oil
4 large eggs
1 cup mini semisweet chocolate chips
1 cup milk chocolate chips
½ teaspoon pure almond extract

Do not preheat the oven. Spray a 12-cup Bundt pan with vegetable cooking spray.

In a large mixing bowl, combine the cake mix, sugar, flour, sour cream, and oil and beat with an electric mixer on low speed just to blend. Add the eggs and blend well. Increase the speed to medium-high and beat for 4 minutes. Fold in all the chocolate chips and stir until they are evenly distributed. Mix in the almond extract.

Pour the batter into the prepared pan and set the oven to 350°F. Bake until a cake tester inserted in the middle of the cake comes out clean, about 55 minutes. Let the cake cool in the pan.

Invert the cooled cake onto a cake plate. The mini semisweet chips will be distributed throughout the cake and the milk chocolate chips will sit near the bottom. Any kind of icing or topping on this cake would be superfluous. Be prepared to serve seconds! MAKES 18 TO 20 SLICES

THE COLLEGE OF
CHARLESTON CAKE

About a year before my husband Billy's death, I told him that I was going to develop a cake for his alma mater, The Citadel, and another one for the College of Charleston, which was Wally's school as well as mine. The idea pleased him. "Just be sure," he said, "that you obtain all the permissions you need." It was fairly easy to start at the College with President Sanders, since his girl friday, Betty Craig, is one of my dearest friends. Thus, the College of Charleston cake quickly became a reality. Sadly, Billy died before the Citadel cake was developed, but the plan has not been abandoned and we hope to soon have our Citadel cake.

The College of Charleston Cake is fashioned after a Toll House cookie. It contains all the ingredients which make Toll House cookies so delicious—brown sugar, nuts, and chocolate chips. Of course, it needs no frosting, but it is especially good with vanilla ice cream for a really special treat.

Shortening and all-purpose flour for greasing the
   Bundt pan
One 18.25-ounce package caramel cake mix (see Note)
⅓ cup firmly packed dark brown sugar

1 cup sour cream
⅔ cup vegetable oil
4 large eggs
1 teaspoon pure vanilla extract
1 cup mini semisweet chocolate chips
1 cup coarsely chopped pecans

Preheat the oven to 350°F. Grease and flour a 12-cup Bundt pan.

In a large mixing bowl, blend the cake mix, brown sugar, sour cream, and oil together with an electric mixer on low speed for 1 minute. Add the eggs one at a time, blending well after each addition. Increase the mixer speed to medium and beat for 4 minutes. Stir in the vanilla extract. Fold the chocolate chips and pecans into the batter with a spatula and stir gently until they are well distributed.

Pour the batter into the prepared pan and bake until a cake tester inserted in the middle of the cake comes out clean, about 50 minutes.

Remove the cake from the oven and allow it to cool in the pan. Invert onto a plate and serve.

MAKES 18 TO 20 SLICES

NOTE: Butter recipe golden cake mix may be substituted for the caramel cake mix.

CHOCOLATE CHIP CAKE

Our Chocolate Chip Cake has become so popular with customers, readers, family, and friends that I've had to promise to include the recipe again in this book. Some people had problems with the temperature and the length of baking time the first time around, so with a few minor changes, here it is again.

Shortening and all-purpose flour for greasing the
  Bundt pan
One 18.25-ounce package butter recipe golden
  cake mix
⅓ cup granulated sugar
One 8-ounce container sour cream (do not use low-fat
  or nonfat)
⅔ cup vegetable oil
3 large eggs
1 teaspoon pure vanilla extract
One 12-ounce bag mini semisweet chocolate chips

Preheat the oven to 350°F. Grease and flour a 12-cup Bundt pan.

In a large mixing bowl, blend the cake mix, sugar, sour cream, and oil together with an electric mixer on low speed for

1 minute. Add the eggs one at a time, blending well after each addition. Increase the mixer speed to medium and beat for 4 minutes. Stir in the vanilla extract. Fold the chocolate chips into the batter with a spatula and stir gently until they are well distributed.

Pour the batter into the prepared pan and bake until a cake tester inserted in the middle of the cake comes out clean, 55 to 60 minutes.

Remove the cake from the oven and allow it to cool in the pan. Invert the cake onto a plate and serve.

MAKES 18 GENEROUS SLICES

THE OBSCENE CHOCOLATE CAKE

Dick Hair is one of our best friends. He is also a real chocolate person. A few years ago, Dick was hospitalized several times and during each recuperation period, we tried to make sure that he had some chocolate to brighten his days. It was during one of these periods that the Obscene Chocolate Cake was born. This is the cake that was created especially for Dick, and he is the one who called it obscene. Chocolate all the way, it's the perfect remedy for any kind of chocolate attack.

Cooking spray for greasing the Bundt pan
One 18.25-ounce package butter recipe golden or
    yellow cake mix
¼ cup unsweetened cocoa powder, sifted
⅓ cup granulated sugar
1 cup sour cream
⅔ cup vegetable oil
4 large eggs
One 12-ounce bag mini semisweet chocolate chips

Do not preheat the oven. Spray a 12-cup Bundt pan with vegetable cooking spray.

In a large mixing bowl, combine the cake mix, cocoa, sugar, sour cream, and oil and beat with an electric mixer on low speed just to blend. Add the eggs and blend well. Increase the speed to medium-high and beat for 4 minutes. Fold the chocolate chips into the batter with a spatula and stir gently until they are well distributed.

Pour the batter into the prepared pan and set the oven to 325°F. Bake until a cake tester inserted in the middle of the cake comes out clean, about 55 minutes. Let the cake cool in the pan for at least 1 hour before slicing.

MAKES 18 TO 20 SLICES

CHRISTMAS CRANBERRY CAKE

Don't ask why we call this cake a Christmas Cranberry Cake. Perhaps we do so because it was created just in time for our holiday brochure a couple of years ago. But the name is misleading since we enjoy it all through the year. It is pretty to see, delicious to eat, and makes a delightful accompaniment to a cup of hot tea.

Cooking spray for greasing the tube pan
3 cups all-purpose flour
1 teaspoon baking powder
1 teaspoon baking soda
1 teaspoon ground nutmeg
1 teaspoon ground cinnamon
½ teaspoon salt
1 cup (2 sticks) butter or margarine, softened
1⅔ cups granulated sugar
4 large eggs
1 cup sour cream
One 16-ounce can whole-berry cranberry sauce
1 cup coarsely chopped pecans or black walnuts

Do not preheat the oven. Spray a 12-cup tube pan or Bundt pan with cooking spray.

Sift together the flour, baking powder, baking soda, nutmeg, cinnamon, and salt into a medium-size mixing bowl. Set aside.

In a large mixing bowl, cream the butter and sugar together with an electric mixer on low speed until creamy, about 5 minutes. Beat in the eggs one at a time, mixing for 1 minute after each addition. Alternately add the sifted dry ingredients and the sour cream. Add the cranberry sauce and beat on low speed until it is well distributed. The batter will become slightly purple. Fold in the nuts with a spatula.

Pour the batter into the prepared pan and set the oven to 350°F. Bake until a cake tester inserted in the middle of the cake comes out clean, 55 to 60 minutes. Let the cake cool in the pan for about 2 hours. Invert the cake onto a serving plate. When the cake is thoroughly cooled, slice and serve. The only accompaniment needed is a fork.   MAKES 20 SLICES

MOCHA CHOCOLATE NUT CAKE

I haven't heard anyone yet who doesn't like this cake. My nephew Lee Gavitt, who lives in Florida and is always glad to see the UPS driver bearing a cake from home, says the Mocha Chocolate Nut is his favorite of all the Charleston Cake Lady cakes. His wife is my niece Teresa Ann. She thinks it is her duty to watch his fat and sugar intake, and she does so with military rigidity. Small wonder then that he is happy to see a cake box arrive, especially when it contains his favorite Mocha Chocolate Nut Cake.

The cake itself is light in texture but the addition of assorted nuts gives it just the right density. Serve it with a scoop of black walnut ice cream or a dollop of whipped cream sprinkled with chopped nuts.

Cooking spray for greasing the Bundt pan
One 18.25-ounce package mocha chocolate cake mix
   (I like to use Duncan Hines)
⅓ cup granulated sugar
1 cup sour cream
⅔ cup vegetable oil
4 large eggs
½ teaspoon pure almond extract

1 cup coarsely chopped black walnuts
½ cup coarsely chopped English walnuts
½ cup coarsely chopped pecans

Do not preheat the oven. Spray a 12-cup Bundt pan with vegetable spray.

In a large mixing bowl, combine all of the ingredients except the nuts. Beat with an electric mixer on low speed until well blended, about 1 minute. Increase the speed to medium-low and beat for 2 minutes. Fold in the nuts with a wooden spoon and mix just until the nuts are well distributed.

Pour the batter into the prepared pan and set the oven to 325°F. Bake until a cake tester inserted in the middle of the cake comes out clean, about 55 minutes. Let the cake cool in the pan. Invert onto a plate and serve.   MAKES 18 SLICES

THE VICTORIA CAKE

In January 1996, shortly after an exhausting holiday baking season, I received a call from Ann Levine of Victoria *magazine, expressing an interest in our cakes. At her request we sent a chocolate chip cake, and within a few days, Kim Freeman called to set up a photo shoot. She and Toshi Osuki came to see us in February. They spent the day taking pictures, and in spite of my not wanting to be photographed, we had a most delightful day. Two more charming people I have never met. They brought with them a request from the editors of* Victoria *for a cake made in honor of their magazine. We created the cake and they loved it!*

Since I couldn't remember ever having tasted a cake from the Victorian Era, I didn't know where to start. Wally suggested the library and that's where I found the lemon sponge idea. Since sponge cake doesn't have a long shelf life and probably wouldn't have traveled well, I tried using a lemon cake mix for a starter. Adding cream cheese and mandarin oranges gave the cake the taste that I figured Victorian-era people would have liked. So far, I've not heard of anyone who doesn't like it. Even the non-lemon lovers like it.

The day spent with Kim and Toshi was one of the Charleston Cake Lady's most pleasant. For Sadie and me it was a lovely day, not to be forgotten. I have had some delightful telephone visits with Ann Levine and look forward to each call. Our cakes

and book were recently featured by her in the Victoria *newsletter,
and we can't keep up with the orders.*

Kudos to Ann, Toshi, and Kim!

Cooking spray for greasing the Bundt pan
½ cup coarsely chopped pecans
One 8-ounce package cream cheese, softened
One 18.25-ounce package lemon supreme cake mix
⅓ cup granulated sugar
2 tablespoons all-purpose flour, unsifted
⅔ cup vegetable oil
4 large eggs
One 11-ounce can mandarin oranges, well drained

Do not preheat the oven. Spray a 12-cup Bundt pan with vegetable cooking spray. Sprinkle the nuts evenly over the bottom of the pan. Set aside.

In a large mixing bowl, cream the cream cheese until it is softened, 1 to 2 minutes. Add the cake mix, sugar, flour, and oil and beat with an electric mixer on low speed just to blend. Add the eggs and blend well. Increase the mixer speed to medium-high and beat for 2 minutes. Add the drained oranges and beat on the lowest speed until the orange pieces are well distributed, 1 to 2 minutes.

continued

Pour the batter into the prepared pan and set the oven to 325°F. Bake until a cake tester inserted in the middle of the cake comes out clean, 45 to 50 minutes. Let the cake cool in the pan. Invert onto a pretty plate and serve.

MAKES 18 SLICES

BROWNIES, CHEWS, *and*

OTHER TAKE-ALONGS

Brownies have always been my downfall, so this is my favorite chapter. I hope you will find something here that will become one of your favorites.

There are a number of brownie recipes in the next few pages. While I won't talk about each one, I must direct your attention to the Designer Brownies. They're just so delicious and rich that I can't talk about them without wishing for one. I recently had the honor of serving some of my goodies at the Chapter Two Book Store's moving celebration. Although Pat

Conroy was the major attraction, Patricia Raad's Designer Brownies caused quite a stir.

I also must explain why the Charleston Chews are mentioned again, since they were published in *Treasured Recipes*. My good pal John Martin Taylor (Hoppin' John) says he always includes his cornbread recipe in every book he writes because it is always in demand. While we are certainly not in Hoppin' John's league, we continue to receive requests for Charleston Chews. So it's here—one more time.

You don't want to miss Mary Michael's lemon squares. Actually, it isn't wise to miss any of her offerings since everything she bakes is delicious!

No excuses now. With all the easy recipes in the following pages you can be the star of any party, picnic, church supper, or even a Pat Conroy book signing!

CHARLESTON CHEWS

For almost forty years, we have been enjoying our Charleston Chews. They really need no improvements or additions since they have stood the test of time. We continue to receive more requests for and raves about this recipe than for any other. So in keeping with my promise, here's the recipe again.

Cooking spray for greasing the cake pan
4 large eggs
One 16-ounce box dark brown sugar
2½ cups self-rising flour, sifted
1 teaspoon pure vanilla extract
1 cup coarsely chopped walnuts or pecans
Sifted confectioners' sugar for dusting

Preheat the oven to 350°F. Grease a 13 × 9-inch pan.

In a large mixing bowl, mix the eggs, brown sugar, flour, and vanilla together with an electric mixer on low speed until well blended. Fold in the nuts with a wooden spoon.

Pour the batter into the prepared pan. Bake until golden brown on top, about 25 minutes. Sprinkle the chews with confectioners' sugar. Cut into squares when cool.

MAKES THIRTY-SIX 2 × 1 ½-INCH SQUARES

WASHINGTON STATE
BROWNIES

These brownies are so rich they could probably qualify for the candy family, too. Using all the goodness of peanut butter, peanuts, marshmallows, and chocolate frosting, the topping can almost stand alone. Combining the topping with the brownie mixture makes an incredible confection. These are super rich, so be sure to serve small pieces.

Our thanks go to Linda Hardy of Auburn, Washington. Linda called and offered me her recipe after she had read Treasured Recipes. *I'm so glad to have had such a generous offer.*

FOR THE BROWNIES
Cooking spray for greasing the cake pan
1 cup all-purpose flour, sifted
2 cups granulated sugar
6 tablespoons unsweetened cocoa powder
¼ teaspoon salt
4 large eggs
1 cup (2 sticks) butter or margarine, melted and cooled
1 teaspoon pure vanilla extract

3 heaping tablespoons crunchy peanut butter
One 6-ounce container milk chocolate frosting
2 cups miniature marshmallows

Preheat the oven to 350°F. Grease a 13 × 9-inch pan.

Mix the flour, sugar, cocoa, and salt together in a medium-size mixing bowl. Set aside. In a large mixing bowl, beat the eggs with an electric mixer on low speed, then add the cooled butter and vanilla. Slowly add the dry ingredients. Mix just until well blended. Do not overmix.

Pour the batter into the prepared pan and bake until a cake tester inserted in the center of the pan comes out clean, 20 to 25 minutes.

Mix the peanut butter with the chocolate frosting and set aside. When the brownies are done, remove them from the oven and cover the brownies with the miniature marshmallows. Return the pan to the oven until the marshmallows are soft and spreadable. Distribute the soft marshmallows evenly, using a spatula. Put spoonfuls of the frosting mixture randomly on the marshmallows and swirl lightly. Refrigerate until the entire mixture is cooled and set. Cut into squares.

MAKES FORTY-EIGHT 1 1/2-INCH SQUARES

DESIGNER BROWNIES

Don't even consider making these brownies unless (a) you're a real chocolate person, and (b) you're willing to spend a little more money than usual. They are, without a doubt, the most delicious brownies I've ever tasted, so I don't mind the higher cost—and apparently I don't worry about the calories either.

This is another one of those fabulous recipes shared with us by Patricia Raad. I think it's her best yet!

Cooking spray for greasing the cake pan
Two 22.5-ounce packages brownie mix (I use Betty
   Crocker Supreme Brownie Mix)
⅔ cup water
⅔ cup vegetable oil
4 large eggs
Three 7-ounce Symphony Milk Chocolate Bars with
   Almonds and Toffee Chips

Preheat the oven to 350°F. Grease a 13 × 9-inch pan.

In a large mixing bowl, using a wooden spoon, mix together 1 package of the brownie mix, ⅓ cup of the water, ⅓ cup of the oil, and 2 of the eggs. Stir gently until the mixture is well moistened.

Pour the batter into the prepared pan. Place the three Symphony Bars, side by side, on top of the brownie mixture.

Using the same bowl, mix the second package of brownie mix with the remaining $\frac{1}{3}$ cup water, $\frac{1}{3}$ cup oil, and 2 eggs. Stir gently until the mixture is well moistened. Pour the batter into the pan on top of the Symphony Bars. Place the pan in the oven and bake until a cake tester inserted in the center comes out clean, about 35 minutes. If it is necessary to increase the baking time, do so in 5-minute increments, checking for doneness after each additional bake time. Let cool in the pan for several hours before cutting.

This is an extremely rich confection, so be sure to serve small pieces. Store in an airtight container up to 10 days.

MAKES FORTY-EIGHT 1-INCH SQUARES

MILK CHOCOLATE CHEWS

Being the chocolate fanatic that I am, I decided to add some chocolate to our famous Charleston Chews. Here is my altered recipe, along with its altered name, Milk Chocolate Chews. They contain just enough chocolate to ward off a chocolate attack.

Cooking spray for greasing the cake pan
½ cup (1 stick) butter or margarine, melted
One 16-ounce box light brown sugar
4 large eggs
2¼ cups self-rising flour, sifted
3 tablespoons unsweetened cocoa powder, sifted
1 teaspoon pure vanilla extract
1 cup coarsely chopped walnuts or pecans
1 cup milk chocolate chips

Preheat the oven to 350°F. Grease a 13 × 9-inch pan.

In a large mixing bowl, mix the melted butter and brown sugar together with a wooden spoon. Add the eggs one at a time, stirring well after each addition. Add the flour and cocoa and mix until the ingredients are well distributed. Stir in the vanilla. Fold in the nuts and chips. Combine well.

Pour the batter into the prepared pan and bake until a cake tester inserted in the center of the pan comes out clean, about 30 minutes. Let cool in the pan, then cut into squares.

MAKES THIRTY-SIX 2 × 1 1/2-INCH CHEWS

KILLER BROWNIES

My niece Teresa Ann and her coworkers at the Daytona Dental Lab take credit for naming the Killer Brownies. Their theory: these brownies are sinfully rich, they're addictive, and one should beware! Perhaps after you have eaten a few, you will agree with their choice of name. I'm sure you will agree to serve very small pieces!

Cooking spray for greasing the cake pan
One 22.5-ounce package brownie mix
⅓ cup water
⅓ cup vegetable oil
2 large eggs
1 teaspoon pure vanilla extract
Three 5-ounce Cadbury Milk Chocolate Bars with
   Roasted Almonds

Preheat the oven to 350°F. Grease an 8 × 8-inch pan, or if you have an oblong pan approximately 10 × 6½ inches, that works exceptionally well.

In a medium-size mixing bowl combine the brownie mix, water, oil, and eggs according to the package directions. Stir in the vanilla.

Pour half the batter into the prepared pan. Cover the batter with the Cadbury Bars. (They will fit in an oblong pan without cutting them. If you use a square pan, break the candy so that the pieces cover the batter.) Pour the remaining batter over the chocolate candy. Bake until a cake tester inserted in the center comes out clean, about 30 minutes. Allow to cool in the pan for at least 1 hour. When thoroughly cooled, cut into 1-inch squares.

MAKES 36 VERY THICK SQUARES

COBBLESTONE BROWNIES

These fall in the nobody-can-eat-just-one category. It takes eating several of them to analyze the three kinds of chocolate since they blend so well together. They're delicious, easily made, quickly baked, and they have never met a stranger who didn't like them.

Cooking spray for greasing the cake pan
One 22.5-ounce package brownie mix (Betty Crocker
    Supreme brownie mix)
⅓ cup water
⅓ cup vegetable oil
2 large eggs
1 teaspoon pure vanilla extract
½ cup milk chocolate chips
½ cup white chocolate chips
½ cup coarsely chopped pecans or walnuts

Preheat the oven to 350°F. Lightly grease a 13 × 9-inch pan.

In a medium-size mixing bowl, combine the brownie mix, water, oil, and eggs according to the package directions. Add the vanilla. Gently stir in both chocolate chips and fold in the nuts.

Pour the batter into the prepared pan and bake until a cake tester inserted in the center comes out clean, 20 to 25 minutes. Allow to cool at least 30 minutes before cutting into squares.

MAKES THIRTY-SIX 2 1/2-INCH SQUARES.

LEMON CHESS PIE SQUARES

Mary Michael insists that when a recipe is "stolen," the food tastes so much better. So, in her capacity as recipe thief, she managed to obtain these little lemon delicacies that melt in your mouth and do wonders for your dessert tray.

FOR THE BOTTOM LAYER
Cooking spray for greasing the cake pan
One 18.25-ounce package lemon cake mix
½ cup (1 stick) butter or margarine, melted
1 large egg

FOR THE TOP LAYER
One 8-ounce package cream cheese
One 16-ounce box confectioners' sugar
3 large eggs

Preheat the oven to 325°F. Grease a 13 × 9-inch pan.

To make the bottom layer, in a large mixing bowl, combine the cake mix, butter, and egg and blend well. Pat this mixture evenly into the prepared pan. Set aside.

To make the top layer, in a medium-size mixing bowl, mix the cream cheese, confectioners' sugar, and eggs and beat with an electric mixer on medium speed until the mixture is creamy, about 3 minutes. Pour the cream cheese mixture over the cake mixture and bake until a cake tester inserted in the center comes out clean, 40 to 45 minutes. Let cool in the pan, then cut into small squares.

MAKES FORTY-EIGHT 1 $\frac{1}{2}$-INCH SQUARES

TASTY MORNING TREATS

Breakfast used to be a big meal in my family. Daddy was raised on a farm, and his idea of breakfast included bacon and/or sausage, eggs, grits, and toast or biscuits. He was the breakfast chef in our family and that was our morning menu. It scarcely ever changed, and if it did, we asked why. These country morning breakfasts suited Billy Pregnall just fine, so when we married, our menu didn't change.

After Daddy's first heart attack, all sorts of things changed, breakfast being one of the first. Daddy was never willing to give up his grits and eggs, but he didn't mind the Egg Beaters, and he reluctantly accepted Dr. Ford Rivers's suggestion to substitute Canadian bacon for the regular bacon and sausage that he dearly loved. So we managed—we changed. Now, we scarcely ever have those wonderful breakfasts. Of course we miss them, but we've learned to enjoy our breakfast treats, as Billy used to call them.

Wally always preferred a breakfast bread, sweet roll, or muffin breakfast, so most of the recipes in this chapter were created with him in mind. I'm especially happy to share them with you.

We try to keep some of these tasty morning treats in our freezer since they make lovely gifts. To make them freezer safe, I wrap them in several layers of plastic wrap, making sure that no air is trapped inside, and put them in an airtight container before freezing them. This way, they enjoy a good freezer life and are ready for us to enjoy or use as gifts. Wrapped in an attractive basket or protected in a small tin, all these little treats need is a colorful ribbon to brighten someone's day. Mini baskets, colorful cellophane bags, and small tins can be found in "dollar" stores.

I hope you will enjoy these Tasty Morning Treats as much as the Pregnall family does.

OATMEAL MUFFINS

There is no more satisfying breakfast bread than an oatmeal muffin.
Stir up a batch while the family is getting ready for work or school.
Then listen to the "ohs" and "ums" when they come to the table.

Shortening for greasing the muffin pan
⅓ cup butter or margarine, softened
½ cup firmly packed dark brown sugar
1 large egg
1 cup buttermilk
1 cup quick-cooking oats
1 cup self-rising flour, unsifted
½ teaspoon baking soda
1 teaspoon pure vanilla extract
1 small apple, left unpeeled, cored, and finely chopped

Preheat the oven to 400°F. Grease a 12-cup muffin pan or insert paper muffin cups.

In a medium-size mixing bowl, mix the butter, sugar, and egg together with a wooden spoon until well mixed. Stir in the buttermilk. Stir in the oats, flour, and baking soda. Stir in the vanilla and fold in the apple.

Pour the batter into the prepared muffin cups and bake until the muffins are nicely browned, 18 to 20 minutes. Remove from the pan and serve warm.

MAKES 12 MUFFINS

PINEAPPLE-PECAN BREAD

For a not-too-sweet breakfast bread, this one gets a high rating.
It is really one of my breakfast favorites because it's just that—
not real sweet. The crushed pineapple and chopped pecans blend
well for a tasty morning treat.

Shortening and all-purpose flour for greasing the
  loaf pan
1¾ cups all-purpose flour
½ teaspoon baking powder
¼ teaspoon baking soda
¼ teaspoon salt
½ cup (1 stick) butter or margarine, softened
½ cup granulated sugar
2 large eggs
½ cup buttermilk
1 cup canned crushed pineapple in unsweetened
  pineapple juice, well drained
½ cup coarsely chopped pecans

Preheat the oven to 350°F. Grease and flour a 9 × 5-inch loaf
pan.

Sift together the flour, baking powder, baking soda, and
salt into a medium-size mixing bowl and set aside.

In a large mixing bowl, beat the butter and sugar together with an electric mixer on medium speed until the mixture is light and fluffy, about 5 minutes. Add the eggs, one at a time, beating well after each addition. Alternately add the dry ingredients and the buttermilk. Stir in the crushed pineapple and the chopped pecans.

Pour the batter into the prepared pan and bake until a cake tester inserted in the center comes out clean, 55 to 60 minutes. Let cool in the pan and slice.   MAKES 10 SLICES

Variation

If your family prefers a sweeter breakfast treat, add the following topping mixture before baking:

2 tablespoons butter or margarine, melted
2 tablespoons firmly packed dark brown sugar
2 tablespoons all-purpose flour, unsifted
¼ teaspoon ground cinnamon

In a small mixing bowl, combine all the ingredients. Sprinkle the topping evenly over the pineapple-pecan mixture before baking.

STRAWBERRY BREAD I

Since I had always eaten strawberry preserves as a spread on my bread, I was surprised to fall heir to a recipe with the preserves in the bread. We tried it; we liked it; and this particular strawberry bread has become one of our special breakfast treats.

Shortening and all-purpose flour for greasing the
   loaf pans
3 cups all-purpose flour
1 teaspoon salt
½ teaspoon baking soda
½ cup sour cream
½ cup (1 stick) butter or margarine, softened
1½ cups granulated sugar
1 teaspoon pure vanilla extract
1 teaspoon fresh lemon juice
4 large eggs
1 cup strawberry preserves
½ cup coarsely chopped black walnuts

Preheat the oven to 350°F. Grease and flour two 9 × 5-inch loaf pans.

Sift together the flour and salt into a small mixing bowl and set aside. Dissolve the baking soda in the sour cream. Set aside.

In a large mixing bowl, blend the butter, sugar, vanilla, and lemon juice together with an electric mixer on low speed. Beat in the eggs one at a time, beating after each addition. Add the sour cream mixture. Blend well. Stir in the flour mixture, then the strawberry preserves, with a wooden spoon. Fold in the nuts.

Pour the batter into the prepared pans. Bake until the bread pulls away from the pans, 35 to 40 minutes. Let cool in the pans before slicing. MAKES 20 GENEROUS SLICES

STRAWBERRY BREAD II

Don't be fooled! This is no ordinary bread. Since it is difficult to decide whether to serve myself a slice of strawberry bread for breakfast or have it for my lunchtime dessert, I invariably have it both times. Alone or adorned with whipped cream, this light, moist confection draws raves every time it is served.

Shortening and all-purpose flour for greasing the
   loaf pans
3 cups all-purpose flour
3 teaspoons ground cinnamon
1 teaspoon salt
1 teaspoon baking soda
2 cups granulated sugar
1¼ cups vegetable oil
4 large eggs, beaten
Two 10-ounce packages frozen strawberries, thawed
   and cut into bite-size pieces, juice included
1 cup coarsely chopped pecans

Preheat the oven to 350°F. Grease and flour two 9 × 5-inch loaf pans.

Sift the flour, cinnamon, salt, and baking soda together into a large mixing bowl. Add the sugar. Stir in the oil, eggs, and strawberries, including their juice. Mix well. Gently fold in the nuts.

Pour the batter into the prepared pans and bake until a cake tester inserted in the center of the pans comes out clean, 60 to 65 minutes. Allow the loaves to cool thoroughly in the pans before slicing.   EACH LOAF MAKES 10 SLICES

NOTE: This recipe is taken from the Bishop England High School cookbook, *Gracious Goodness . . . Charleston*, one of the best collections of unusual and exciting recipes I've ever seen.

SADIE'S APPLESAUCE MUFFINS

Although our housekeeper, Sadie, is considered "the boss" in our household, as well as among our relatives and friends, she claims she doesn't like the title at all. So we have given her a new title, and she says she likes it much better. She's now the "Muffin Lady," and this recipe for applesauce muffins is one of her favorites. She excels in the muffin department, so I know you will enjoy the recipes she shares with us.

Shortening for greasing the muffin pan
2 cups all-purpose flour
1 teaspoon baking soda
1½ teaspoons ground cinnamon
1 cup granulated sugar
1 large egg
½ cup (1 stick) butter or margarine, melted
1 cup applesauce
1 teaspoon pure vanilla extract
1 cup coarsely chopped pecans or walnuts (optional)

Preheat the oven to 375° F. Grease a 12-cup muffin pan or insert paper muffin cups.

Sift all the dry ingredients together into a large mixing bowl. Add the egg, melted butter, and applesauce. Stir with a wooden spoon until well mixed. Stir in the vanilla. Fold in the nuts.

Pour the batter into the prepared pan and bake until a cake tester inserted in the center of each muffin comes out clean, 15 to 20 minutes. Serve warm or at room temperature. They're delicious any way you serve them! MAKES 12 MUFFINS

PEACH MUFFINS

A muffin that serves as breakfast food and equally well as bread at dinner is a bonus. So here's a bonus. These peach muffins are not too sweet and contain just a hint of cinnamon, exactly the right amount. Peach is one of my favorite muffins, the kind I like to keep in my freezer.

Several of these muffins placed in a little basket and tied with a pretty ribbon makes a special homemade gift.

Shortening for greasing the muffin pan
1 cup peeled, pitted, and chopped fresh peaches
1 teaspoon fresh lemon juice
1 cup milk
1 large egg
¼ cup (½ stick) butter or margarine, softened
⅔ cup granulated sugar
2 cups all-purpose flour
3 teaspoons baking powder

Preheat the oven to 350°F. Grease a 12-cup muffin pan or insert paper muffin cups.

Sprinkle the peaches with the lemon juice and set aside.

In a large mixing bowl, mix the milk, egg, butter, and

sugar together with a wooden spoon. Sift in the flour and baking powder and mix well, then fold in the peaches.

Pour the batter into the prepared pan, filling each cup two-thirds full. Bake until the muffins are lightly browned on top, about 20 minutes. Remove from the pan and serve warm or at room temperature.   MAKES 12 MUFFINS

NOTE: Canned peaches may be used. Drain well and omit the lemon juice.

YOGURT MUFFINS

I have a long-standing idea that yogurt or sour cream in baked goods almost automatically creates a winner. So far, my idea hasn't been too far off, and these yogurt muffins stand as proof. They're easy to make, fairly healthy, and they are oh-so-good!

Shortening for greasing the muffin pan
1 cup whole-wheat flour
½ cup all-purpose flour
1 teaspoon baking powder
1 teaspoon baking soda
⅓ cup granulated sugar
½ teaspoon ground cinnamon
½ cup fruit (blueberries, chopped peeled apple, or
   chopped peeled pear)
⅓ cup coarsely chopped pecans
⅓ cup butter or margarine, melted
One 8-ounce container lemon yogurt (you may
   substitute the flavor of your choice)
1 large egg

Preheat the oven to 350°F. Grease a 12-cup muffin pan or insert paper muffin cups.

In a medium-size mixing bowl, sift together the flours, baking powder, baking soda, sugar, and cinnamon. Add the fruit and nuts and mix. Add the butter, yogurt, and egg and stir with a wooden spoon just until the mixture is moistened.

Pour the batter into the prepared pans and bake until the muffins are nicely browned, 18 to 20 minutes. Serve warm or cold.   MAKES 12 MUFFINS

SPECIAL BRAN MUFFINS

Bran muffins have been around for many years. They're whole-some, fairly healthy, and very few folks dislike them. But how many times do we hear rave reviews over a simple bran muffin? Not often. So we added one more ingredient, and our bran muffins have become special. Extremely moist and delicious, these versatile muffins are good anytime. We like them for break-fast, but they fit well in the bread basket at any meal.

Shortening for greasing the muffin pan
2 cups bran cereal (I use All-Bran)
1¼ cups milk
1¼ cups all-purpose flour
½ cup granulated sugar
1 tablespoon baking powder
½ teaspoon salt
¼ cup canola oil
2 large egg whites
½ cup strawberry applesauce

Preheat the oven to 400°F. Grease a 12-cup muffin pan or insert paper muffin cups.

In a large mixing bowl, combine the bran cereal and milk. Let this mixture stand for 5 to 10 minutes.

Sift together the flour, sugar, baking powder, and salt into a small mixing bowl. Set aside. To the cereal mixture add the oil and egg whites and mix well with a wooden spoon. Stir in the dry ingredients. Add the strawberry applesauce and stir until all of the ingredients are combined. Do not beat.

Divide the batter into the 12 muffin cups. Bake until lightly browned, about 20 minutes. Serve warm or cold.

MAKES 12 DELICIOUS MUFFINS

PINEAPPLE COFFEE CAKE

A few years ago, Wally was involved in a traffic accident, and that's how we were introduced to the Pineapple Coffee Cake. Wally's car was hit by a car driven by Helen Williams, a "senior" lady who failed to stop for a red light. Thankfully, no one was hurt—only the cars were damaged, both badly. This dear little lady was so upset to have ruined Wally's sports car and he was so concerned for her well-being that they became fast friends. On one of her subsequent visits she brought the Pineapple Coffee Cake for us to taste. We thought the taste, the cake, and the lady were all just great.

Note that this cake contains neither eggs nor shortening, yet it is extremely moist and rich. We serve it for breakfast, but it goes equally well on the dessert bar with a spoonful of vanilla ice cream or a dollop of whipped cream.

Cooking spray for greasing the cake pan
2½ cups all-purpose flour
1 teaspoon baking soda
½ teaspoon baking powder
½ teaspoon salt
1½ cups granulated sugar
¼ cup firmly packed light brown sugar
⅓ cup coarsely chopped pecans
One 20-ounce can crushed pineapple in its own juice

Preheat the oven to 350°F. Spray a 9-inch springform pan with cooking spray.

Into a large mixing bowl, sift together the flour, baking soda, baking powder, and salt. Stir in the sugars. Add the nuts and stir with a wooden spoon until the ingredients are well distributed. Add the pineapple and juice. Stir gently just until moistened. Do not overmix.

Pour the batter into the prepared pan. Bake until a cake tester inserted in the center of the cake comes out clean, 50 to 55 minutes. Let cool for 10 minutes. Loosen the cake from the edge of the pan with a knife or spatula. Release the side of the pan and allow the cake to cool thoroughly before slicing.

MAKES 10 TO 12 SLICES

PUMPKIN CRANBERRY BREAD

Although this bread is usually baked in two loaf pans, I bake it in a round "novelty" pan (see Note), and because it looks as good as it tastes, it draws raves every time. Even though no shortening is used, the bread is extremely moist. It is delicious alone, but for a special treat, serve it with softened cream cheese.

Shortening and all-purpose flour for greasing the
  loaf pans
2¼ cups all-purpose flour
2 teaspoons baking power
½ teaspoon salt
2 large eggs
2 cups granulated sugar
1¾ cups canned pumpkin (*not* pumpkin pie mix)
1 cup dried cranberries (they're sometimes sold as
  Craisins)

Preheat the oven to 350°F. Grease and flour two 9 × 5-inch loaf pans.

Sift together the flour, baking powder, and salt into a medium-size mixing bowl. Combine the eggs, sugar, and pumpkin in a large mixing bowl. Blend with an electric mixer on low speed for 1 minute. Add the dry ingredients and beat on low speed just until the ingredients are blended. Fold in the dried cranberries.

Pour the batter into the prepared pans and bake until a cake tester inserted in the center comes out clean, 55 to 60 minutes. Let cool in the pans and slice.   MAKES 20 SLICES

NOTE: My novelty pan is from Williams-Sonoma. It is called a festive pan.

THE "EXTRA-GOODS"

THIS CHAPTER, THOUGH QUITE SHORT, contains all the recipes that are extra-good and not to be missed. You will definitely want to try Maureen Frye's Pistachio Pie, and you should not pass up the ultradelicious Layered Dessert (my favorite). There are also two more greats from our recipe thief—Mary Michael's Chocolate Chip Walnut Pie and her Bread Pudding.

They are all *extra-good*.

MARY MICHAEL'S
BREAD PUDDING

Let's all hope that Sadie doesn't see this recipe. It doesn't resemble her bread pudding, but it's oh-so-good. It's another one of Mary Michael's stolen items, with her touch added, so we know it's good. In fact, it's much better than good—and served with Bourbon Sauce, it's superb.

Cooking spray for greasing the cake pan
One 16-ounce loaf day-old raisin bread
½ cup dark raisins
1 teaspoon ground cinnamon
1 teaspoon ground nutmeg
¾ cup (1½ sticks) butter or margarine, melted
2 cups granulated sugar
4 large eggs
1 quart milk
Bourbon Sauce (recipe follows)

Preheat the oven to 350°F. Lightly grease a 13 × 9-inch pan.

Break the bread into small pieces and place in the pan. Mix in the raisins, cinnamon, nutmeg, and butter. In a large mixing bowl, mix together the sugar and eggs with a wooden spoon. In a small saucepan, heat the milk over medium heat until it is not quite boiling. Pour the hot milk into the bowl and mix well with the sugar and eggs. Pour this mixture over the bread mixture in the pan. Let it set until the bread soaks up the milk.

Cover the pan with a sheet of aluminum foil and bake for 30 minutes. Remove the foil and bake 30 minutes more. Remove the bread pudding from the oven and allow it to cool for 30 minutes. Top with Bourbon Sauce and serve.

MAKES 12 SERVINGS

Bourbon Sauce

1 cup confectioners' sugar
2 large eggs
½ cup (1 stick) butter or margarine, melted
Bourbon to taste

In a medium-size mixing bowl, beat the sugar and eggs together with a wooden spoon. Add the melted butter and mix well. Add the bourbon, stir, and serve with the Bread Pudding.

PISTACHIO PIE

Of my many new friends, Maureen Frye is a very special one. On a trip to Charleston from Hatboro, Pennsylvania, Maureen called to order a cake for her son and to ask if I'd autograph her copy of Treasured Recipes. *What a delightful lady she is. We had a most enjoyable visit that day, and since then we have kept in touch. I wish Hatboro wasn't so far away!*

Maureen has shared some of her family recipes with us, and I'm happy to share this one with you. It's her family's favorite summer pie. We like it so well we don't wait for summer to enjoy it!

One 3¾-ounce package instant pistachio pudding mix
1 pint vanilla ice cream, softened
¾ cup milk
One 9-inch graham cracker pie crust
One 4-ounce container frozen whipped topping,
    thawed
One 1³⁄₁₆-ounce bar English toffee candy, crushed

In a large mixing bowl, combine the pudding mix, ice cream, and milk. Beat with an electric mixer on medium speed until the mixture is smooth and blended well. Pour the mixture into the pie crust and freeze for 1 hour.

Spread the whipped topping evenly over the pie. Sprinkle the crushed candy bar over the whipped topping and return the pie to the freezer. Before serving, allow the pie to sit at room temperature for 5 to 10 minutes.

MAKES 8 GENEROUS SLICES

DESSERT MADE EASY

Have you ever received word that "extras" are coming for dinner? Or have you ever wished you had an extra-special dessert for the bridge club ladies? Well, here it is. You can put this together quickly, easily, and with items you probably have in your pantry. Try it, just once—you won't be sorry!

Cooking spray for greasing the cake pan
2¼ cups all-purpose flour
1½ cups granulated sugar
4½ teaspoons unsweetened cocoa powder
1½ teaspoons baking soda
¾ teaspoon salt
1½ teaspoons white distilled vinegar
1½ teaspoons pure vanilla extract
½ cup plus 1 teaspoon vegetable oil
1½ cups cold water
One 16-ounce container frozen whipped topping,
    thawed

Preheat the oven to 325°F. Grease or spray the bottom of a 13 × 9-inch pan with cooking spray.

Sift all of the dry ingredients together into the prepared pan. Scoop out three holes in the mixture. Add the vinegar to one hole, the vanilla to the second hole, and into the third hole pour the oil. Pour the cold water over the mixture and stir with a wooden spoon. Bake until a cake tester inserted in the center of the pan comes out clean, 30 to 35 minutes. Let the cake cool in the pan. When it is thoroughly cooled, cut the cake vertically into three sections. Loosen the sides and bottom with a large spatula (I use an egg turner for this). Place the first section on a cake plate. Cover the cake with one-third of the thawed topping, then place the second section on the top, cover with another third of the topping, and proceed until the three sections are in place and the whole cake is covered with topping. Refrigerate until serving time.

MAKES 12 TO 15 LARGE SLICES

NOTE: This creation is not only rich and sinful, it looks elegant. I usually serve it on an oblong plate, earning it the name "oblong torte" from one of my friends. I insist that it's Dessert Made Easy—but don't tell your guests just how easy it is.

LAYERED DESSERT

There is no more delicious dessert anywhere than this one, believe me. It may seem like a lot of work but it really isn't.

FOR THE CRUST

Cooking spray for greasing the cake pan
½ cup (1 stick) butter or margarine, melted
1 cup all-purpose flour, unsifted
¼ cup firmly packed dark brown sugar
¾ cup coarsely chopped pecans

FOR THE FILLING

One 8-ounce package cream cheese, softened
¾ cup granulated sugar
1 teaspoon pure vanilla extract
One 8-ounce container frozen whipped topping, thawed

FOR THE TOPPING

Two 3¾-ounce packages instant lemon pudding
3 cups cold milk
One 8-ounce container frozen whipped topping, thawed

Preheat the oven to 350°F. Spray a 13 × 9-inch baking pan with cooking spray.

In a small mixing bowl, mix the butter, flour, sugar, and pecans together, creaming well. Pat this mixture into the prepared pan and bake for 15 minutes. *Do not overbake.* The crust will be soft when it is first removed from the oven. It will become crusty when it cools.

To make the filling, in a medium-size mixing bowl, blend the cream cheese and sugar together with a wooden spoon. Mix well. Add the vanilla and the thawed whipped topping and mix well. Spread this mixture over the crust.

To make the topping, in a medium-size mixing bowl, mix the instant lemon pudding and milk together, stirring until well blended. Place this mixture over the filling in the pan. Finish the dessert by spreading the frozen whipped topping over the top. Chill for several hours before cutting into serving pieces. MAKES TWENTY-FOUR 2-INCH SQUARES

CHOCOLATE CHIP
WALNUT PIE

Mary Michael insists that desserts taste better when the recipe is "unlawfully obtained" or, as she often says, "It's much better if I steal the recipe!" So here is the second of two more gems from our lovable recipe thief. This Chocolate Chip Walnut Pie is unbelievably easy to make and it literally melts in your mouth.

1 cup semisweet chocolate chips
$\frac{2}{3}$ cups coarsely chopped walnuts
1 unbaked 10-inch pie shell
1 cup dark corn syrup (I use Karo brand)
$\frac{1}{4}$ cup light corn syrup (I use Karo brand)
2 large eggs
2 tablespoons butter or margarine, melted

Preheat the oven to 350°F. Place the chocolate chips and walnuts in the bottom of the pie shell. In a medium-size mixing bowl, mix together the dark and light corn syrups, the eggs, and the butter. Pour this mixture over the chocolate chips and walnuts and bake for 40 minutes. Serve warm or cool.

MAKES 8 GENEROUS SLICES

IN ANN'S MEMORY

Ann Stender Gilmore was a true friend to many people. I was one of those lucky ones. Because her friendship was so special to me, I've asked some of her closest friends to help me dedicate a short chapter to her memory. The recipes on the next few pages are presented by some of her closest friends—Mary Ann Cotten Nelson, Ann Boniface Molony, Joan Walsh Evans, and Joan Hartnett Budds—women who have known Ann for more years than any of them care to remember and have loved her as much as I have.

We all miss Ann. She was indeed a dear friend.

MARY ANN NELSON'S
APPLE SQUARES

Mary Ann claims that she is not a baker, yet everything that comes from her oven is mouthwatering good. Her apple squares are a prime example. They're rich enough for any dessert bar, but they also find a place of honor on the breakfast tray. And they are super easy to make.

Cooking spray for greasing the cake pan
2 cups all-purpose flour
2 teaspoons baking powder
½ teaspoon salt
½ teaspoon ground cinnamon
1 cup firmly packed dark brown sugar
1 cup granulated sugar
½ cup (1 stick) butter or margarine, melted
2 teaspoons pure vanilla extract
2 large eggs, slightly beaten
1 cup cored and chopped unpeeled apples
1 cup coarsely chopped pecans or walnuts

Preheat the oven to 350°F. Grease a 13 × 9-inch pan.

Sift all of the dry ingredients into a large mixing bowl and mix well with a wooden spoon. Stir in the butter, vanilla, and eggs and mix well. Stir in the apples and nuts.

Pour the batter into the prepared pan and bake until lightly browned on top, 30 to 40 minutes. Allow to cool before cutting into squares.

MAKES FORTY-EIGHT 1 1/2-INCH SQUARES

ANN MOLONY'S
CHRISTMAS TARTS

Ann serves these wonderful confections at all of her parties, especially her holiday parties, and we all look forward to them. Truly one of life's little culinary treasures, they are so delicious that you will find yourself serving them all year and wondering why she calls them Christmas tarts.

FOR THE SHELLS
- ½ cup (1 stick) butter, softened (do not substitute margarine)
- One 3-ounce package cream cheese, softened
- 1 cup all-purpose flour, unsifted

FOR THE FILLING
- ½ cup (1 stick) butter, softened (do not substitute margarine)
- 1 cup granulated sugar
- 2 large eggs, separated
- 2 teaspoons pure vanilla extract
- 1 cup golden raisins
- 1 cup coarsely chopped pecans

To make the shells, in a small mixing bowl, cream together the butter and cream cheese. Gradually add the flour and form into a ball. Refrigerate overnight.

To make the filling, in a medium-size mixing bowl, mix the butter and sugar together with a wooden spoon until well mixed. Separate the eggs and add the yolks to the bowl. Stir in the vanilla, raisins, and nuts. In a separate medium-size mixing bowl, beat the egg whites with an electric mixer on high speed until stiff peaks form. Add the beaten egg whites to the filling mixture and fold in gently.

Preheat the oven to 325°F. Have four small ungreased muffin or tart pans ready.

Don't remove the entire batter from the refrigerator at once. Pinch off a section and place it on a clean, hard surface. Flour the surface. With a rolling pin, roll the batter to a thickness of $1/8$ inch. With a small glass or a cookie cutter, cut the batter into circles approximately 3 inches in diameter. Place the circles in the ungreased pans and fill two-thirds full with the filling. Bake for 30 minutes. Remove the tarts from the pans and let cool on a rack.   MAKES 48 TARTS

JOAN EVANS'S
FORGOTTEN COOKIES

Joan's Forgotten Cookies are highly recommended by all who have ever tasted them. They are called "forgotten" because you place them in the oven and forget about them overnight. These little dainties are probably the lightest cookies I have ever eaten. They literally melt in your mouth, so be prepared to have plenty of them on hand when you begin serving.

Cooking spray for greasing the cookie sheets
4 large egg whites
1½ cups granulated sugar
1 cup semisweet chocolate chips
2 cups coarsely chopped pecans

Preheat the oven to 350°F. Grease two 14 × 12-inch cookie sheets.

In a large mixing bowl, beat the egg whites with an electric mixer on high speed until thick and foamy. Gradually add the sugar. Beat until the mixture is stiff and holds peaks. Fold in the chocolate chips and pecans with a wooden spoon.

Drop the batter by teaspoonfuls onto the prepared cookie sheets. Place the cookie sheets in the preheated oven, turn the oven off, and leave the cookies overnight in the oven. Stored in an airtight container, these cookies will stay fresh for one week.　MAKES 48 COOKIES

JOAN BUDDS'S PINEAPPLE REFRIGERATOR CAKE

The inclusion of this recipe is special since it comes from someone who is not well. Joan's health has been poor for some time, so it was doubtful that one of her recipes could be obtained for us. Ann Molony's husband, Raymond, suggested that since these "girls" had been close friends since they were five years old, he suspected that Ann might have Joan's recipe for Pineapple Refrigerator Cake. Ann did! And we are all fortunate since it is a spectacular dessert. It's light, it's delicious, it's extremely popular, and it serves a big crowd.

Cooking spray for greasing the cake pan
One 18.25-ounce package yellow or white cake mix
One 20-ounce can crushed pineapple, undrained
1 cup granulated sugar
One 5⅝-ounce package instant vanilla pudding mix
1 cup sour cream
One 12-ounce container frozen whipped topping, thawed
Sweetened grated coconut (optional)
Chopped walnuts or pecans (optional)

Preheat the oven to 350°F. Grease a 13 × 9-inch pan.

Prepare the cake mix according to package directions and bake in the prepared pan. While the cake is baking, combine the undrained pineapple and the sugar in a medium-size saucepan and heat until the mixture boils. Boil for 2 minutes and set aside. When the cake is done, remove it from the oven and pierce the entire top of the cake with a fork. Pour the pineapple mixture over the hot cake and allow the cake to cool.

Prepare the pudding according to the package directions and fold in the sour cream. Spread this mixture over the cooled cake. Top with the whipped topping. Sprinkle with grated coconut and/or chopped nuts, if desired. Store in the refrigerator or serve immediately.   MAKES 24 SERVINGS

INDEX

Air Force apple pound cake,
    16–17
Ann Molony's Christmas tarts,
    116–17
apple:
    in oatmeal muffins, 83
    pound cake, Air Force, 16–17
    squares, Mary Ann Nelson's,
        114–15
    in yogurt muffins, 94–95
applesauce muffins, Sadie's,
    90–91

Beer cake, 28–29
Betty Rivers's rum cake,
    43–44
blackberry jam cake, 26–27
blueberries, in yogurt muffins,
    94–95
bourbon sauce, in Mary Michael's
    bread pudding, 104–5

bran muffins, special, 96–97
bread:
    pineapple-pecan, 84–85
    pumpkin cranberry,
        100–101
    strawberry I, 86–87
    strawberry II, 88–89
bread pudding, Mary
        Michael's, 104–5
brownies:
    cobblestone, 76–77
    designer, 70–71
    killer, 74–75
    Washington State, 68–69
buttermilk pound cake,
        Sumama's, 18–19

Charleston chews, 67
chews:
    Charleston, 67
    milk chocolate, 72–73

chews (*continued*)
    Roberta Josey's Savannah,
    41–42
chocolate:
    cake, heavenly, 50–51
    cake, obscene, 56–57
    chews, milk, 72–73
    marbled pound cake, 8–9
    mocha nut cake, 60–61
    pound cake, white, 12–13
    see also brownies; German
    chocolate
chocolate chip(s):
    cake, 54–55
    in cobblestone brownies,
    76–77
    in College of Charleston
    cake, 52–53
    in heavenly chocolate cake,
    50–51
    in Joan Evans's forgotten
    cookies, 118–19
    in milk chocolate chews, 72–73
    in obscene chocolate cake,
    56–57
    walnut pie, 112
Christmas:
    cranberry cake, 58–59

cobblestone brownies, 76–77
coconut:
    in German chocolate pound
    cake, 4–5
    in Margaret Wilkes's
    graham cracker nut cake,
    37–38
    in orange marmalade cake,
    24–25
    -pecan-topped German
    chocolate cake, 32–34
coffee cake, pineapple, 98–99
College of Charleston cake,
    52–53
cookies, Joan Evans's
    forgotten, 118–19
cranberry:
    cake, Christmas, 58–59
    pumpkin bread, 100–101
cream cheese:
    in Anne Molony's Christmas
    tarts, 116–17
    icing, in pineapple sheet
    cake, 30–31
    in layered dessert, 110–11
    in lemon chess pie squares,
    78–79
    in *Victoria* cake, 62–64

Dates:
    in beer cake, 28–29
    in Roberta Josey's Savannah
        chews, 41–42
designer brownies, 70–71
dessert made easy, 108–9

Eggnog cake, 48–49
evaporated milk pound cake,
    14–15

German chocolate:
    cake, coconut-pecan-topped,
        32–34
    pound cake, 4–5
graham cracker nut cake,
    Margaret Wilkes's, 37–38

Heavenly chocolate cake, 50–51

Ice cream, in pistachio pie,
    106–7

Joan Budds's pineapple
    refrigerator cake, 120–21
Joan Evans's forgotten cookies,
    118–19
Joyce McCarrell's buttermilk
    pound cake, 20–21

Killer brownies, 74–75

Layered dessert, 110–11
lemon:
    chess pie squares, 78–79
    pudding, in layered dessert,
        110–11
    7UP pound cake, 10–11
    Victoria cake, 62–64

Marbled pound cake, 8–9
Margaret Wilkes's graham
    cracker nut cake, 37–38
marshmallows, in Washington
    State brownies, 68–69
Mary Ann Nelson's apple
    squares, 114–15

Mary Michael Hair's pecan
praline cake, 39–40
Mary Michael's bread pudding,
104–5
milk chocolate chews, 72–73
mocha chocolate nut cake,
60–61
muffins:
oatmeal, 83
peach, 92–93
Sadie's applesauce, 90–91
special bran, 96–97
yogurt, 94–95

Nut(s):
graham cracker cake,
Margaret Wilkes's, 37–38
mocha chocolate cake, 60–61
pistachio pie, 106–7
in Roberta Josey's Savannah
chews, 41–42
see also pecan(s); walnut(s)

Oatmeal muffins, 83
obscene chocolate cake, 56–57

orange(s):
mandarin, in *Victoria* cake,
62–64
marmalade cake, 24–25

Peach muffins, 92–93
peanut butter, in Washington
State brownies, 68–69
pear, in yogurt muffins, 94–95
pecan(s):
in Ann Molony's Christmas
tarts, 116–17
in beer cake, 28–29
in Betty Rivers's rum cake,
43–44
in Charleston chews, 67
in Christmas cranberry cake,
58–59
in cobblestone brownies,
76–77
-coconut-topped German
chocolate cake, 32–34
in College of Charleston
cake, 53–54
in eggnog cake, 48–49
in German chocolate pound
cake, 4–5

in Joan Evans's forgotten
cookies, 118–19
in layered dessert, 110–11
in Margaret Wilkes's graham
cracker nut cake, 37–38
in Mary Ann Nelson's apple
squares, 114–15
in milk chocolate chews, 72–73
in mocha chocolate nut cake,
60–61
-pineapple bread, 84–85
in pineapple coffee cake, 98–99
in pineapple sheet cake, 30–31
praline cake, Mary Michael
Hair's, 39–40
in Sadie's applesauce
muffins, 90–91
in strawberry bread II, 88–89
in *Victoria* cake, 62–64
in yogurt muffins, 94–95
pie:
chocolate chip walnut, 112
pistachio, 106–7
pineapple:
coffee cake, 98–99
in Margaret Wilkes's graham
cracker nut cake frosting,
37–38

-pecan bread, 84–85
refrigerator cake, Joan
Budds's, 120–21
sheet cake, 30–31
pistachio pie, 106–7
pound cake, 1–21
Air Force apple, 16–17
evaporated milk, 14–15
German chocolate, 4–5
Joyce McCarrell's
buttermilk, 20–21
marbled, 8–9
Sadie's choice, 6–7
7UP, 10–11
Sumama's buttermilk,
18–19
white chocolate, 12–13
praline pecan cake, Mary
Michael Hair's, 39–40
pumpkin cranberry bread,
100–101

Raisins:
golden, in Ann Molony's
Christmas tarts, 116–17
in Mary Michael's bread
pudding, 104–5

Roberta Josey's Savannah
chews, 41–42
rum cake, Betty Rivers's, 43–44

Sadie's applesauce muffins,
90–91
Sadie's choice pound cake, 6–7
7UP pound cake, 10–11
special bran muffins, 96–97
strawberry bread I, 86–87
strawberry bread II, 88–89
Sumama's buttermilk pound
cake, 18–19

Tarts, Ann Molony's
Christmas, 116–17

Victoria cake, 62–64

Walnut(s):
in Air Force apple pound
cake, 16–17
in beer cake, 28–29

in blackberry jam cake, 26–27
in Charleston chews, 67
chocolate chip pie, 112
in Christmas cranberry cake,
58–59
in cobblestone brownies, 76–77
in Mary Ann Nelson's apple
squares, 114–15
in milk chocolate chews,
72–73
in mocha chocolate nut cake,
60–61
in Sadie's applesauce
muffins, 90–91
in strawberry bread I, 86–87
Washington State brownies,
68–69
whipped topping, frozen:
in dessert made easy, 108–9
in Joan Budds's pineapple
refrigerator cake, 120–21
in layered dessert, 110–11
in pistachio pie, 106–7
white chocolate pound cake,
12–13

Yogurt muffins, 94–95